An Unusual Self-Help Book

How I Discovered The Secret of Success In The Bible

BY CLINTON DAVIDSON

How I Discovered The Secret of Success In The Bible

by Clinton Davidson

* * *

2020 Edition Published by

The Davidson Family

Copyright © 2020
Michael Menes Publications
All Rights Reserved

ISBN 978-1-6541059-2-1

* * *

Originally Published by

FLEMING H. REVELL COMPANY

Westwood, New Jersey

1961

Library of Congress Catalog Card Number: 61-13621

Cover Image by

Blank & Stoller Photography

c. 1927

Michael Menes
PUBLICATIONS

"The basic principles of human relationships never change. That is one thing that we must fix firmly in our minds. Methods may change. Emphasis may change. Products may change. The market may change. But the fundamental principles of salesmanship and good business never change one iota. What was right three thousand years ago is right today. That is what makes the Bible different from all other books of the world, whether those books are on religion, science, salesmanship, or any other subject. The Bible was right when it was first written and is still right today. That is why anyone in this world with normal intelligence, and industry enough to apply himself to the task, can succeed by simply following the principles laid down in the Bible."

- Clinton Davidson

Clinton Davidson
(1888 ~ 1967)

Photo by Bruno Hollywood c.1955

ABOUT THE AUTHOR

CLINTON FRANKLIN DAVIDSON was born in Atlanta, Georgia on October 15th, 1888, the son of Daniel and Frances (Hitt) Davidson, a family of German, Scottish and Irish decent. He was only two years old when his alcoholic father, who had been engaged in the business of advertising, tragically committed suicide using a straight razor. Clinton lived in poverty during much of his childhood with his mother and sister in Louisville, Kentucky where he received only an 8th grade public education. In 1901 and 1902 Clinton attended the Potter Bible College in Bowling Green, Kentucky sponsored by members of the Church of Christ. James A. Harding, the president of Nashville Bible School (now Lipscomb University) had been given land, a building and financial support by Clinton and Mary Potter in memory of their son. At the new school in Bowling Green, Harding and his faculty taught the Bible, Greek and other subjects. This was Clinton Davidson's only formal education.

Early Years Working in Finance

In order to help support his family, at 14 years of age Clinton became an assistant shipping clerk for the Louisville Cement Company until 1904 when he started working as a bookkeeper with the Fidelity Columbia Trust Co. He was promoted to savings account teller and later to the trust department. He resigned in 1912 to become an agent for the Mutual Benefit Life Insurance Company in Louisville. In 1918 he became a general agent for the Connecticut Mutual Life Insurance Company and in 1920 he moved to Buffalo, New York where he sold life insurance with Connecticut Mutual until 1925. During this time he was reputed to have written more life insurance each year for eight consecutive years than any other agent in the field and made life insurance history by selling ten million dollars of life insurance in a single year. By 1923, he had gained considerable knowledge concerning the investment of wealth and that year coined the phrase *Estate Planning*. Aside from the work to support his family, from 1908 to 1917 Clinton preached at the Sellersburg Church of Christ in Sellersburg, Indiana.

In 1925, beginning with only two New York City clients, he

relocated to Manhattan and organized The Estate Planning Corporation for the purpose of providing advisory services to wealthy clients' investments and estates. Through writing letters to other wealthy people and offering them customized financial advice concerning investments and taxes, he grew his business until by 1950 it planned the estates of approximately 400 clients whose combined wealth amounted to over four billion dollars. These clients included Alfred P. Sloan, Marshall Field, Pierre Cartier, Charles W. Hook, and seven branches of the du Pont family.

Fiduciary Counsel and Oil & Gas Companies

When the stock market crashed in October of 1929, Mr. Davidson spent a year investigating many forms of investment management. He determined through this inquiry that financial institutions managing personal trust funds did not practice sufficient statistical or economic research. He concluded that the fees derived from small investment accounts were not sufficient to cover the costs of both the individual attention required by them and economic research.[1] Subsequently, in 1931 he founded Fiduciary Counsel, Inc. which engaged primarily in economic research. He served as chairman of Fiduciary Counsel until his retirement in 1964. Over these years he extended these services to corporations as well. By 1945 these corporate clients included approximately 100 of the leading industrial and merchandising companies of the United States. In 1939, Mr. Davidson was solely responsible for the recapitalization of Marshall Field & Co. He also negotiated the purchase and sale of several leading industrial corporations.

Between 1950 and 1960 he raised 25 million dollars for oil and gas exploration and development. He organized several companies for this purpose including The Oil & Gas Co., Mineral Projects Inc., Mineral Ventures Corporation, Oil & Gas Ventures Inc., and Davidson & Hartz Inc.

Influencing Government Spending & Tax Legislation

Clinton Davidson contributed articles to insurance and banking journals as well as *"THIS WEEK* in Washington," a column that was

---

[1] The National Encyclopedia of American Biography

carried in 900 newspapers across America in the 1950's. As a master salesman and authority in fiduciary, financial and tax matters, he was often asked to help "sell ideas" to politicians in Washington appearing as an expert witness before the United States House of Representatives Ways and Means Committee and the finance committee of the U.S. Senate. He originated, presented, and carried through to enactment seven tax bills, one of which resulted in the federal government refunding five billion dollars to corporations. He also wrote sixteen pieces of testimony that after the end of the Second World War controlled the settlement of all war contracts. Many of the bills passed by Congress in this area were written in Mr. Davidson's office. He was the author of four additional books on finance and taxation held in the Library of Congress, including "The Hazards of An Unprotected Estate" (1928), "Minimizing Taxes and Avoiding Capitol Losses in Estates" (1929) and "Keeping Purchasing Power Intact" (1938).

Support of Christian Colleges, Camp Shiloh & The Church of Christ

Clinton, with his wife Flora Davidson, took great interest in supporting Camp Shiloh through establishing the Church Contribution Trust. This charity helped make available a 64-room building and thirty-eight acres of land in New Jersey to provide recreation for underprivileged children from the inner city neighborhoods of New York City. By 2019, this charitable organization had touched the lives of over 10,000 inner city youth since 1951. Although now relocated to New York State, it continues to serve inner city youth and change lives at the time of this publication. Clinton and Flora also founded *The Wildwood Church of Christ* and for two years published *The Christian Leader* to encourage optimism in the Church of Christ during the Great Depression era.

In the 1930's, feeling an obligation to pay back a debt for the things he had learned from James A. Harding[2] and John Nelson Armstrong at Potter Bible College, Clinton played a key role in raising and donating funds to save Harding College. He aided George S. Benson, the second president of the university, to eliminate the debts through his network of wealthy business clients and fundraising techniques. One of the major contributors was George Pepperdine of Pepperdine University,

---

[2] See History of the Restoration Movement: James A. Harding

the founder of Western Auto Supply Company. Clinton Davidson received honorary LL.D. degrees (the highest academic law degree) from Harding College in 1938 and from Pepperdine University in 1961. One historian noted that had the Church of Christ had a clergy, Clinton Davidson would have had a status similar to a bishop. He was affiliated with the Stone-Lipscomb tradition, defended his allies in the church during the premillennialist controversy and helped shape the direction of the Church of Christ during the 20th century.[3] He gave speeches at Abilene Christian University and other schools and sponsored many friends and family members to earn degrees at Christian colleges. With Pat Boone he helped purchase the Morris Clothier estate in Villanova, Pennsylvania and started Northeastern Christian Junior College in 1957 before it merged with Ohio Valley College in 1993.

Defending the Free Market System

Clinton's association and support of George Benson's work helped propel the nation's emerging conservative political movement. George Benson, who had spent a decade in China as a Christian missionary, established the National Education Program[4] (NEP) in 1941. The NEP promoted *Americanism* over the course of four decades, warning Americans about the growing threat of Communism. *Americanism* upheld three fundamental principles: belief in God, belief in the U.S. Constitution and belief in the free-enterprise system. This alliance with Harding University and the NEP helped Ronald Reagan rise in the ranks of the Republican Party landscape. In 1962, Reagan collaborated with George Benson on the historic film *"The Truth About Communism"* and in 1981, Benson would be nominated for the Presidential Medal of Freedom.

Even with all these achievements during Clinton Davidson's career, he avoided boasting of his accomplishments. The many things he achieved, he thought possible only through the strength he found in reading the Bible and by serving his Lord. Politically, he was a pacifist and a small government Republican conservative who reached out to both

---

[3] See *Reviving the Ancient Faith*: The Story of Churches of Christ in America by Richard T. Hughes

[4] See Encyclopedia of Arkansas: National Education Program

sides of the aisle and stood strongly for the American free-enterprise system.

Family Life & Balbrook

Married to Flora Davidson for 57 years, they had one son, Clinton Davidson, Jr. Their son was a mathematician and economics professor at Harding College with a degree in economics from Yale. Clinton Davidson Jr. later became the CEO of Washington based Resort Airlines, the largest private sector carrier of military cargo in the 1950's. Resort Airlines also specialized in holiday travel to Cuba, Haiti and the Dominican Republic. From the 1930's to the 1970's, the Davidsons lived on their 250 acre Balbrook estate in Mendham, New Jersey and left four grandchildren who had five great grandchildren. Clinton Davidson passed away at the age of 78 at his home in 1967.

FORWARD

In 1967, when I was 5 years old, my great grandfather, Clinton Davidson, suffered a sudden heart attack which abruptly ended his life at the age of 78. I have no memories of my great grandfather. However, his contribution to the lives of everyone in my family was extraordinary.

At that young age, my parents had purchased six acres of land on the corner of the Davidson's 250 acre Balbrook estate in Mendham, New Jersey. There, they built a home for us to be close to the grandparents. As kids growing up, we had unlimited access to the enormous property my great grandparents owned in the Somerset Hills of New Jersey. It was a very different place back then. We built tree houses, swam in the lakes, raced homemade box cars down the estate roads and when we got older discovered how off-road motorcycles were the best way to explore endless trails and paths around Balbrook and beyond. We played with the children of the families my great grandmother, Flora Davidson, had rented several homes to on the estate. Balbrook was its own community.

In the summers, Flora Davidson would host the inner city kids on the estate from Camp Shiloh, a Christian charity that brought children from the inner city to experience what the Davidsons referred to as *"real American living"* in the countryside just forty miles outside of Manhattan. With my sister and my younger brother, we'd catch the school bus each morning at the stone gates of Balbrook and after school, we'd get dropped off and visit our great grandmother. She had become confined to a wheel chair on the third floor of the Balbrook mansion. Having fallen and broken her hip some time before my great grandfather had left us, she would tell us the story of how she was cured of horrible pain through prayer. We would visit her often and my sister would play her Steinway grand piano in the room on the first floor with two enormous portraits of Clinton and Flora hanging on the wall next to the fireplace. On the third floor there was one office filled with typewriters and file cabinets, left just how my grand grandfather had left it. Another office had photography and film equipment with machines for cutting film together and a dark room for photography. And there were bookshelves and books everywhere. *What a mansion it was!* Every Christmas, Flora would hold an enormous Christmas dinner in a room with a fabulous chandelier and invite all our relatives to attend. The rule every year at these occasions was to *never* serve any alcohol whatsoever at Balbrook. Alcohol was strictly forbidden. As kids growing up it was all 'normal' and it never occurred to us to ask too many questions. In hindsight, it was indeed an extraordinary childhood, thanks to this mysterious unknown person, Clinton Davidson.

If all this wasn't enough, there was another mansion called Shiloh which bordered Balbrook. It had been purchased and organized with large support by my great grandparents to serve religious purposes. Whenever we would explore Shiloh, we would feel like we were the children of royalty. We were never 'trespassers.' We would attend Sunday school and church services at Shiloh regularly. I recall seeing a magician for the first time and a trick using milk that dripped down the elbow of a volunteer plucked from the audience. Later, in studying the history of the Restoration Movement in America which led to the founding of the Churches of Christ, I would learn that giving credibility to things that are supernatural was accepted. When I learned that my great grandfather would tell spooky Halloween stories to all the grandchildren, and roll around on the floor consumed in belly laughs after he delivered the big scare, the pieces of the puzzle fit so perfectly together. Or when my mom told me that the Shiloh mansion was haunted because a caretaker had committed suicide up in the attic and that a ghost had been seen more than once… Belief in the supernatural helped in teaching the stories of the Bible!

Flora Davidson in Mendham, New Jersey at Balbrook

When my Great Grandmother, Flora, passed away in 1980, she left us with a trust fund. I knew little of how the money was earned, only that my great grandfather had been "a businessman." It was not until I was in my fifties with a true appreciation of what it takes to earn a living, that I began asking my mother deeper questions about my great grandfather. She confided in me by saying, "Your great grandfather was a very *interesting* man." My mother is not someone to exaggerate and always made every effort to be truthful. Later she told me that she and her brother, Frank, were raised very strictly and to tell a lie was "the worst crime." If you told a lie, you would get a severe spanking, or a lashing with a belt if you were a boy as did my uncle at times. The discipline was intense. If you were a kid, anything with an *"ing"* at the end, was not permitted at Balbrook. She added, "Your great grandfather was a *natural* salesman. He could sell *anything* to *anyone*. He was a *master*." She later added, "And he had a great sense of humor." Knowing that my mother never exaggerated, this made me very curious and my sister and I began to research Clinton Davidson and how he made his fortunes in life.

Flora and Clinton Davidson (seated) with Clinton Davidson, Jr. (left) and fiancé Gene Rosamond Davidson (right) on the Atlantic City Boardwalk in the 1920's. Photo courtesy of the Davidson Family.

We discovered that he had written six books that were in the Library of Congress in Washington, D.C. One of those books, *How I Discovered The Secret of Success In The Bible*, provided an amazing collection of instructions on how to be a great salesman and shared an incredible life story that we were largely unaware of. In addition, because the principles had been extracted from Biblical stories, the book offered timeless advice based on the unchanging understanding of human nature that Clinton Davidson discovered in the Bible. This foundation makes his book about discovering financial success (and success in life) just as powerful today as it was when it was written over a half century ago. Clinton wrote his book during his retirement after he had already made his great fortunes, not as a means to promote himself or his career (as some do) but as a book that might help others succeed.

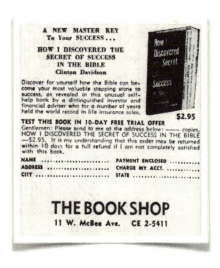

Original newspaper advertisement from 1961.

Additional research into what made his mind tick led us to a treasure trove of historical figures and rich ideology. Because he didn't have a father, Clinton Davidson likely found in James A. Harding a father figure who was a man with extraordinary faith in God, a man who crisscrossed America by horse and wagon and established churches wherever he preached. This intersection of faith, business, politics, finance, and rugged individualism is where my great grandfather made his mark in life. His writings contain masterful words on salesmanship, persuasiveness, how to win people over through honesty, hard work and perseverance, and most of all to appreciate the wisdom of the good book.

    It has been my privilege and honor to restore this forgotten yet intriguing self-help book written by my great grandfather, Clinton Davidson.

Michael S. Menes

October, 2019

WHY THIS BOOK WAS WRITTEN

THIS BOOK IS about a discovery that has brought me a satisfactory share of the good things of life. I am convinced that the same discovery can bring anyone a greater abundance of what he most deeply desires.

People sometimes ask me how I have achieved success. I do not claim to have achieved it. Many men who boast of their accomplishments have really done very little, while those who have accomplished much never believe that they have reached the pinnacle of success. Deep within I know that I have not; many others have done much more.

No, I do not claim success for myself, but i do wish to share the *secret* that I know from many years of personal experience can bring good fortune to those who make use of it. Nothing in this book is theory. All of it has been tested in the proving-ground of life. It works for me and it will work for you.

American history is full of great success stories; so is the Bible. Not necessarily money-success, but thrilling accomplishment through the use of such basic principles as I have set down in this book. May some of that thrill be yours as *you* discover the secret of success.

- Clinton Davidson

To My Wife
Flora

Table of Contents

About the Author	5
Forward	10
Why This Book Was Written	14
Publisher's Note	17
~ Chapter 1 ~ THE GOLDEN KEY TO SUCCESS	18
~ Chapter 2 ~ REACHING THE TOP	29
~ Chapter 3 ~ UNDERSTANDING HUMAN NATURE	47
~ Chapter 4 ~ GETTING PEOPLE TO BELIEVE YOU	56
~ Chapter 5 ~ MAKING THINGS CLEAR	67
~ Chapter 6 ~ HOW TO HANDLE OBSTACLES	75
~ Chapter 7 ~ THE LESSON OF THE PILE DRIVER	86
~ Chapter 8 ~ HOW TO GET THE DECISION YOU WANT	91
~ Chapter 9 ~ BECOME THE GREATEST IN YOUR FIELD	102
~ Chapter 10 ~ BE A ONE-EYED MAN	109
~ Chapter 11 ~ THE POWER OF SUGGESTION	118
~ Chapter 12 ~ MAKING POSITIVE USE OF THE NEGATIVE	130
~ Chapter 13 ~ THE FIGHTING FINISH	139
~ Chapter 14 ~ CAN THE ORDINARY PERSON SUCCEED?	145
~ Chapter 15 ~ DISCOVER YOUR OWN SUCCESS SECRETS	154
Acknowledgements	159
Scrapbook & Photos	160
Links & References	183

PUBLISHER'S NOTE

The dollar values that are quoted throughout
this book should be adjusted for inflation.
For example, in the early 1960's, $100 is equal to
$865 in 2019. $100 in 1935 would be
the equivalent of $1,869 in 2019.

Exact conversions of dollar values can be calculated online.

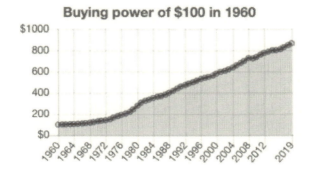

~ CHAPTER 1 ~

THE GOLDEN KEY TO SUCCESS

WHEN I WAS twenty-five years old I was making $35 a month selling life insurance.[1] That doesn't sound like success, does it? In the whole twelve months of my first year as a salesman I earned exactly $420. Even in those days most life insurance salesmen started out earning $200 a month, and it took me five years to make that much.

If you had known me then you might have concluded that I was a born failure. I was shy, retiring - discouraged. When I was two years old my father, an alcoholic, killed himself, and my mother had to go to work in a department store to support my sister and me. For quite a while the three of us lived in one room. Through most of my childhood we moved about among different aunts who took us in by turn.

From those days I can remember what it feels like to be hungry, to have your schoolmates poke fun at you because your clothes don't fit. I developed a real inferiority complex. I can remember one time when the teacher of my fifth grade class asked me to stand up and recite part of the lesson, and I just stood there in front of the class and cried.

---

[1] Born in 1888, Clinton Davidson was twenty-five years old in 1913.

As a boy I had no father, no brothers, no close male relative. I suppose that a psychoanalyst would attribute the inferiority feelings which dogged me into manhood, in major part at least, to this lack of a father figure to identify with in my formative years. I seemed perfectly trained for failure!

When I began selling life insurance I sometimes made forty calls a day - without getting a single interview. At last my boss handed me a stack of blotters imprinted with my name and the company's name and address. "Pass these out," he said. "Go back later to the people you gave them to and you should be able to get *some* interviews and sell some insurance." I tried that but I don't think I averaged one interview a week. I didn't seem to have any ability in salesmanship.

A number of years later a business periodical entitled *The Eastern Underwriter* published the following item:

Life Insurance	Annuities	Total Volume	Premiums Collected
$ 325,000.00	$ 125,000.00	$ 450,000.00	$ 357,600.00
$ 50,000.00		$ 50,000.00	$ 600.00
$ 1,055,000.00	$ 140,000.00	$ 1,195,000.00	$ 370,000.00
$ 500,000.00		$ 500,000.00	$ 16,000.00
$ 825,000.00	$ 400,000.00	$ 1,225,000.00	$ 896,500.00
$ 750,000.00		$ 750,000.00	$ 34,000.00
$ 815,000.00	$ 400,000.00	$ 1,215,000.00	$ 896,500.00
$ 4,320,000.00	$ 1,065,000.00	$ 5,385,000.00	$ 2,571,200.00
$ 1,000,000.00		$ 1,000,000.00	$ 60,000.00
$ 5,320,000.00	$ 1,065,000.00	$ 6,385,000.00	$ 2,631,200.00

The million-dollar case not included in the first total was written and examined prior to January 1 but not issued until after that date.

Other large cases written by this man during the year but not falling in December were four cases with premiums of $1,650,000, one case for $2,100,000.

He led three companies in production.

That record was mine. For seven years I sold more life insurance each year than any other individual in the world. I coined the phrase "Estate Planning." After leaving the life insurance field in 1938, I became president of three corporations, chairman of the board of six, and originator of seven different bills relating to taxation which I presented before the Senate and Congressional committees and saw enacted into law. I raised $25 million for operations resulting in 278 successful oil wells. I formed Fiduciary Counsel, Inc. whose clients' wealth exceeds half a billion dollars. I also founded the Estate Planning Corporation, which during the past thirty-five years has planned the estates of individuals having a total wealth of more than three billion dollars. I published a seventy-year-old national religious magazine for several years and my newspaper column "This Week in Washington With Clinton Davidson" is being carried by approximately 900 newspapers. Among my honored friends is Pat Boone, to whom I am financial and tax adviser. One of my deepest satisfactions is the summer camp on my New Jersey estate. There, each summer, five hundred children of all classes, races, creeds, and colors discover real American living and the love of God.

None of this is mentioned with any thought of boasting. All my life I have had a horror of taking personal credit for what I have been able to do, and I am convinced that what lifted me up out of failure can do just as much for anyone.

What I have accomplished in my work, you can do in the sphere of your ability, whatever it is. In this book are many illustrations from my experience as a salesman, but the basic principles apply to achievement and success in anything. Whether you work in a factory or an office, jerk sodas or teach school, clerk in a store, preach the gospel, raise a family, or whatever you do, you can put to work the secret of success I discovered.

During the past forty-nine years I have been selling not only life insurance, which I did for the first twenty years, but also *ideas*. Selling ideas has involved such projects as raising capital, merging businesses, and persuading multi-millionaires to let me advise them on all their investments. I call this type of selling *"getting people to do what you want them to do."*

From Moses, Jonah, Paul, and other great Bible characters skilled in the power of persuasion, I have learned that getting a person to do what you want him to do is simply a matter of leading his mind up four mental steps. First, you must get favorable *attention*. Second, you must change that attention into real *interest* in the thing you want him to do. Third, you must change that desire into *action*. In the remainder of this book I shall try to show you how I learned from the Bible how to do these four things.

Persuading people to do what you want them to is the utmost importance for everyone. The teenager who wants his parents to let him drive a car, the lawyer who is seeking a verdict for his client, the minister who is trying to influence the people of his parish, the young lady who is seeking a husband: all these, and all who work with people, need to understand these four steps.

In selling life insurance, the first thing I had to learn was how to get *favorable attention*. In other words, I had to get my prospect to want to hear my story. And in that, I was a complete failure until I learned the secret of Apostle Paul.

Saint Paul did such a wonderful job selling his ideas that even today, nineteen hundred years later, at least a billion people have been influenced to some extent by his message. Probably no one ever had more success putting across ideas. And what tremendous obstacles he faced! Whereas I was trying to sell life insurance to people where I lived, Paul was continually traveling from one foreign city to another, a stranger wherever he went. And no missionary society or church supported him; he was on his own, with only the help of God, during a large part of his life. Furthermore, the Apostle Paul had to sell one of the most difficult people who worshiped idols, and he had to persuade them to believe in the God of the Bible. Not only that, but he also had to convince them that this God had an only Son, and that they could be saved from destruction only through that Son.

On top of all that, Paul had terrific opposition. Probably many people in business often think their competition is pretty tough, but Paul's competition was far worse than anything you or I face today. Again and again he was slandered, beaten up, jailed. Once he was stoned, dragged outside the city where he had been preaching, and left for dead. Many times he was at the point of death.

As I studied the life of the Apostle Paul, I asked myself how Paul achieved such overwhelming success in getting people to accept and act on his ideas. I knew what I would have done if I were among people who hadn't even heard of my God and I wanted to introduce them to Jesus Christ. How would I get them interested? If I could find the technique that Paul used it shouldn't be impossible for me to get some of his results.

I read the seventeenth chapter of Acts. Paul was in Athens, a center of learning, religion - and superstition. While walking around the city he had seen many altars, and even one inscribed "To an Unknown God." Standing on Mars Hill, he said in effect, "Men of Athens, I see that in every way you are very religious. For as I passed along observing the objects of your worship, I found an altar with the inscription 'To an Unknown God.' This God who is unknown to you I am here to make known to you."

In one sentence the Apostle Paul tied something he knew his hearers were interested in to the thing he wanted them to become interested in.

"Why don't I do that?" I asked myself. I had been looking at my job from my own point of view and hadn't given much thought to the viewpoint of the fellow I was trying to sell. I would introduce my subject by saying, "I represent the John Hancock Mutual Life Insurance Company." Who was interested in that? No one! But if I could find the thing my prospect was interested in, start with that, and tie it to the thing I wanted him to get interested in...

I had been trying to sell life insurance to men in Goodyear, Goodrich, Firestone, and other tire companies, without success. Now I went back to one of the same men who had refused to hear me the week before. I said, "I want to talk to you about a non-blow-out, puncture proof life insurance policy."

Startled, he asked, "What is that?"

He was asking me to tell him about my product!

I answered, "A man who has bought a certain amount of life insurance usually leaves it to his wife in one lump sum, hoping it will give her an income as long as she lives. But some relative sells her a bad investment, or somebody comes along with some 'blue sky' stock to sell, or she gets into some shaky speculations, and a puncture is put in her income. Before long there are more punctures, and in a few years the whole thing is blown out."

He said, "You are right, there!"

"Now," I said, "It is possible to take the life insurance that you already have, add more insurance to it, and provide and income for your wife of $100.00 a month, and that income will last as long as she lives, and there isn't anything on this earth that can put a puncture in the income or blow out the principal."

I saw that my new approach had attracted his attention - his favorable attention. He said, "Tell me more about it." I got my interview. I had not learned all the steps of salesmanship, but I had learned the first one.

After that, I went to one after another of the tire people and approached them with the same introduction. I tied into my opening sentence the thing that they were interested in and the thing I wanted them to become interested in. I got interviews in every case.

Every man is interested in his own business, so there was no difficulty in finding out what my next prospects were interested in. Every one of them said, "Go ahead. Tell me about it."

There were three partners in one agency that sold trucks. I had been in there before, had talked to one partner, and had tried to get him to let me tell him about a partnership life insurance policy, but he refused to listen. Now, with my new approach, I came back and said, "I want to talk to you about a three-cylinder truck life insurance policy."

He said, "There are no three-cylinder trucks."

I said, "I know that, but there are three partners in your business, and I have a life insurance policy that will take three partners on one policy. Just one piece of paper insure all three, and if one dies the benefits go to the other partners. Did you ever hear of that?"

He said, "No, I never did."

I said, "This policy is just for business purposes. A truck is just for business purposes, isn't it?"

"Yes."

"Well," I said, "That's why I call this a truck, because it is for business purposes. So I call this policy a three-cylinder truck life insurance policy. Would you let me tell you about it?"

He said, "Sure, sit down."

Why did he say that? Because I had followed the winning technique of the Apostle Paul.

I remember one day a man with whom I had an appointment failed to keep it. To fill in the time, I went around looking at the doors on the same floor of the building, and on one door I saw the word "paper." Down at the bottom of the door was "R. Anderson."

I went in. It was a small office. Just one man was there. I said, "Are you Mr. Anderson?"

"Yes." he replied, "What can I do for you?"

I said, "I want to talk to you about a fortune on paper."

"What is that?"

"Oh," I said, "Most people call it a life insurance contract. It is just a piece of paper with some things printed on it, but in most cases it is the only fortune that man has for his old age or is able to leave his family at his death."

He said, "You know, you are right about that - sit down."

This total stranger told me to sit down, because I talked to him about something he was interested in - paper. I tied it to the one thing I wanted to interest him in - life insurance - and I had a successful interview.

As I continued to study the Bible, I found out more about that master salesman the Apostle Paul. He reveals one of his great secrets in his First Epistle to the Corinthians (9:20-22).

"Unto the Jews I became as a Jew," writes Paul, "that I might gain the Jews; to them that are under the law, [I became] as under the law, that I might gain them that are under the law; To them that are without law, as without law… that I might gain them that are without law. To the weak I became the weak, that I might gain the weak: I am made all things to all men, that I might by all means save some."

Why did Paul become like a keeper of the law to those under the law, like a person outside the law when he was among those outside the law? He became all things to all men that by all means he might win some men!

You might call that "getting into the other fellow's shoes." That is one of the first things I had to learn in order to succeed. I had to learn the language of the person I wanted to persuade. More than that, I had to get on his side of the fence, step into his shoes, see through his eyes.

As I began to do this I realized what a service I could render the person who bought one of my policies. Life insurance is the only wealth many persons leave behind. An untaxable inheritance, it can provide for a man's old age at the same time it guarantees that his widow and children will be cared for in the event of his death. Previously I had been trying to sell policies; now, looking through my clients' eyes, I was offering each one an invaluable benefit.

Thus I was able to command the attention of each man I approached because I put myself in his place and felt as he felt. I soon learned, however, that to transform favorable attention into a favorable decision you must know more about your subject than anyone you meet. How to do this is the subject of the next chapter.

~ CHAPTER 2 ~

REACHING THE TOP

When I was fourteen years old I attended a religious school. The president of the school was named James Harding, after whom the famous Harding College is named. President Harding spoke in chapel every morning and I remember many of the things he said. One of them was this: *"Whatsoever thy hand finders to do, do it with they might"* (Ecclesiastes 9:10). Sometimes we change that and say, "A thing worth doing is worth doing well." But the Bible gave us the original idea: Whatever you do, do with all your might. Whatever your work is, put everything you've got into it. Don't go at anything haphazardly, don't scratch the surface, don't give a job part-time attention; give it your best. From the age of fourteen I have repeated that Scripture again and again and again, and it has had a great influence on me.

The great Supreme Court Justice Oliver Wendell Homes, Jr. once called that statement from Ecclesiastes infinitely important. He added: "If you want to hit a bird on the wing you must have all your will in focus, you must not be thinking about yourself, and, equally, you must not be thinking about your neighbor; you must be living in your eye on that bird. Every achievement is a bird on the wing." That is a profound comment.

Another verse President Harding used to emphasize was this: "Seest thou a man diligent in his business? he shall stand before kings; he shall not stand before mean men" (Proverbs 22:29). I took that as a promise directed straight at me, and it sank down into my subconscious mind and made me thorough and painstaking about my work. Later I learned that Benjamin Franklin had known that verse and lived by it. He claimed its literal fulfillment in his life; after amazing success as a businessman and scientist, he stood before the kinds of Europe as the distinguished representative of the government of the United States.

The Bible tells the story of David, the youngest child in his family, who as a boy took care of sheep. If you read the life of David, you will find that he was an unusually good shepherd. Being very diligent in his business, he was taken from the sheepcote and made the king of Israel.

And then there was Joseph. You remember how he was sold as a slave and later put in prison. In every position he held, in everything he did, he was diligent. Whatever he did, he gave everything he had to it. Finally he was taken out of prison and became virtual ruler of the most powerful nation in the civilized world of that time.

Another young man who overcame many obstacles was Daniel. But although Daniel was a slave and was given duties as a slave, he was diligent in those duties. He became the president of the council of Darius and a statesman in three great kingdoms.

President Harding used to say in those chapel talks that had such an influence on my later life that it was just as easy for God to do a big thing as a little thing. As I listened to him I was convinced that that was true, and I was sure that it could be true of me. From Sunday school I knew the stories of Joseph, and David, and

Daniel; when they were young, I felt, they had been no more important than I was, but God had done great things through each of them. I believed that if He wanted to do something big through me, He could do it just as easily as something small.

Soon after I started in the life insurance business, I read in a magazine that an agent in Memphis, Tennessee, had sold a million dollars of insurance in that year. At that time I had sold only $60,000, but I said, "If a man in Memphis can sell a million dollars of insurance in a year, a man in Louisville can. Some day *I'll* sell a million dollars of insurance in a year."

A few years later I learned of a man in Detroit by the name of George Beach who had sold one of the Fisher brothers two million dollars of life insurance in one sale. That was more than I had ever dreamed of. On the other hand, I said to myself: "George Beach is no more a favorite of God than I am. If George Beach can sell two million dollars of insurance to one man, I can sell that much. Not now, but some day." And I did.

When I started selling, the "experts" told me not to study the actuarial side of life insurance, because, they said, "If a man is a good salesman, you don't want to ruin him by making a poor actuary out of him." I wasn't a good salesman, so I did study the actuarial side of life insurance. I wanted to know about the reserves and how they were figured for different policies. I wanted to understand all sides of the business. In studying those items, I found that anyone who had purchased a 20-payment life insurance policy, and had let the dividends accumulate for sixteen years, could use those dividends to make a policy fully paid up immediately. That is, it would be changed from a 20-payment policy to a 16-payment policy. As the owner would not have to pay any more premiums, I could say to him, "Take the money you've been paying and buy a new policy with it." So, having learned that the reserves at the end of sixteen years on a 20-payment life policy, plus the reserves on the accumulated dividends, equaled the reserves on a single-premium policy, I was able to advise my clients in a matter that was for their own benefit. I then looked through the books to find the people who had bought 20-payment life policies sixteen years before in that agency. One of them was an officer of the bank that I had left - the Fidelity Columbia Trust Company. His name was Render. I went to see him and said, "Mr. Render, you have a $5,000 policy in our company and is is possible for you now to have $7,500 of insurance and not pay any more each year than you have been paying."

He said, "That's interesting. How is that?"

So I showed him how he could do it. He said, "Do I have to pass a medical examination?"

I said, "Yes."

He said, "All right, I'll do it."

He was examined, the new policy was issued, and when I delivered it to him, he said, "You know, Clinton, I've been thinking about this. It has been a long time since I've taken any life insurance and I think I ought to have $5,000 more. Can I get it on this same examination?"

The fact that he asked this question proved that I didn't know a thing about selling. A good salesman would have said to himself, "He needs more insurance," and he would have had an additional $5,000 policy issued on approval. But you see I was just the opposite of a salesman, and Mr. Render had to sell *me* on the idea that he should have $5,000 more! Nevertheless, I got him interested, had him examined, and sold him the insurance through having learned something extra about my business.

Almost ten years later, after I had moved to Buffalo, I started trying to sell on what we called the Estate Planning method. I had a man working for me who had been in charge of the trust department of one of the local banks. He called on people, told them how we could help them with their inheritance taxes and their wills, and asked them to give us certain information regarding their estates. He called on a Mr. Cabana who owned three profitable businesses. When my associate had explained his business, Mr. Cabana said, "All right, but you will have to get the information from my controller. I suggest you come in and see him next Tuesday." When he saw the controller on Tuesday, he secured and brought back all the things we asked for, and in the papers there was a note from the boss to the controller which read: "Dear Fred, These people are experts on income tax. Give them everything they ask for."

We were not experts on income tax. We didn't know anything about income tax and we didn't tell anyone we did; he got it mixed up. We had talked to him about the *inheritance* tax. When I read the note, I said to myself, "If being an expert on income tax will get wealthy people to give you all the information you ask for, I'll become an expert on income tax."

So I bought some books on income tax and I stayed up many times until two o'clock in the morning studying. After I had gone through those books and had a general idea of income tax, I then employed the leading tax accountant and the leading tax attorney in Buffalo on a consulting basis to teach me about income tax. Later on, I did become an expert on income taxes, but I doubt if I ever would have been if I hadn't found that note to "Dear Fred." There was a branch of my business about which I knew nothing, but just as soon as a prospect taught me that it was a very important branch, I determined to find out something about it.

Several years after this, our representative called upon a successful Chicago man to explain the use of a certain type of trust. The prospect didn't believe our representative and said, "No, that isn't so." I was asked to call on the prospect and I did. After a while he said, "Now, I want to ask you a real question."

He asked me the question about income tax that he had asked our Chicago representative. I gave him the answer and he said, "Now there you're wrong." He then read a letter from his attorney which contradicted my statement. He also mentioned that his attorney's father was then a Justice of the United States Supreme Court.

"Well," I said, "your attorney has overlooked the latest decision on the subject. If you don't mind calling your stenographer in, I'll dictate a letter to you and, if you send the letter to him, I'm sure he'll tell you I'm right about it." So I dictated the letter stating that I had read his letter to his client and that I assumed he had overlooked the latest decision on the question and I felt certain that he would write back to Mr. B. and explain the matter to him. Of course, it looked rather egotistical for a fellow who was not a lawyer to tell a client that his attorney was wrong and then ask his attorney to admit it.

I came back the next week and he received me with open arms. He said, "You know, the most amazing thing has happened. My attorney said just exactly what you said. He wrote me stating that he had overlooked the latest decision and that you were absolutely right." Later our Chicago representative said, "Clinton, if you were to tell Mr. B. to jump out the seventh story window, I believe he would jump out! From now on he'll do anything you ask him to do."

I am no longer in the Estate Planning division of our business. Mr. Hartz succeeded me and as President he has the reputation wherever he goes that whatever he says about Estate Planning is right and whatever suggestions he makes are the right things to do. It is recognized that whatever he does, he does thoroughly. He is not a surface scratcher. Any young man who approaches his business with that viewpoint and works at it for twenty years will become successful in his field.

A successful man to whom I sold a million dollars' worth of insurance had been an officer in a very steady business for thirty years, and the business seemed rather monotonous to him. He wanted to get into something with more glamour. Some of the people in his city sold him an amusement park. He called me and said, "Clinton, I have never done anything since you became my agent without having you go over it. I bought this amusement park while you were away. The sellers retained a half-million-dollar mortgage, but the mortgage is made through a corporation, thereby relieving me of all personal liability. I want you to look over the sales contract for me."

I replied, "I'm not a lawyer."

He said, "I know you're not a lawyer, but nevertheless I've been following your advice, and I want you to examine the contract."

I read the sales contract and said, "Who told you that you yourself do not have that half-million-dollar liability?"

He said, "My attorney, the former owners, and their attorney."

"Well," I said, "if I can read, it says here that you are personally liable."

He said, "Oh, no! No! That couldn't be! My own attorney told me I'm not. I couldn't have that liability. It might make me penniless."

"Well," I said, "let me write you a letter and tell you that it appears to me that you are liable, and ask you to have your attorneys explain to you why you are not."

So I wrote him that letter. He took it to his attorneys, and they looked at it and said, "You are liable, but it's too late now. The contract has already been signed."

I said to him, "If you tell them you are going into court, and stand pat on it, the contract will be changed." It took him about two months, but he did get it changed.

Did I know more about a sales contract than the lawyers who drew it up? No, did not. Why was it that this man and his attorneys didn't see what I saw in that contract? This man had been a good businessman for thirty years. Then he and his wife became social climbers, and about nine-tenths of his time was devoted to society. He ceased giving everything he had to his business. He didn't observe the contract carefully; he just looked at the surface. His lawyers were equally careless. Every employer finds out that many of the people he employs aren't interested in thoroughness. They are happy to go along carelessly, thoughtlessly; they are just surface scratchers.

Every once in a while I'm accused by some people of being a good salesman. They say, "Oh yes, Clinton can do so and so because he is a natural salesman." Actually, I never got anything because I was a good salesman or because it was easy. Every accomplishment has meant hard work."

I got started in New York by sending out letters with cards for the prospects to return, requesting me to deliver a book. A man I shall call Mr. Brown returned one of those cards. I delivered a book and told him that I thought I could help him, but I would need to get quite a bit of information. He said, "You go over to Paul B. Warner & Company, my accountants, and if they approve of it, they will get the information for you."

I did, and while talking to them, I asked them about the insurance Mr. Brown had purchased. They explained that the had sold a portion of his business to the XYZ Stores Company and in the transaction a new corporation had been formed. The new corporation had issued $2,600,000 of preferred stock, one-half to Mr. Brown and one-half to the XYZ Stores Company. The by-laws or resolutions required two things. First, that every dollar of income that could be used to pay off the preferred stock should so be used; and second, that Mr. Brown's life should always be insured for the full amount of the stock outstanding, which at the start was $2,600,000.

I got the information that I needed. I spent several days full time studying it over, and I well remember that while sitting in front of the fire at night going over it, I found in the by-laws or resolutions that the insurance must be purchased on the basis that represented the least cash outlay, so that all possible cash could be used to retire the preferred stock. My head began churning around asking, "What is the least cash outlay?" The type of insurance that was purchased was called 5-year term. It was good for only five years and, therefore, the premium was very low. My thoughts were going around and around trying to find a way to get a lower cash outlay. That was the key to the whole thing. I finally worked out a plan. Two yearly premiums on the insurance had been paid. If Mr. Brown changed this low premium insurance into high premium insurance, dating the new policies back two years, the insurance companies would lend the money to pay the difference.

You are probably asking, "What difference did that make?" By using the loan and paying interest on it, he was paying interest instead of paying premiums. His company could use the interest as a deduction against taxable income, thereby making a large income tax saving, but no such deduction could be used by paying premiums. Because of tax saving on the interest, the new plan resulted in lower cash outlays each year.

I explained this to the treasurer of the company. He said, "No, that can't be. It just doesn't make any sense. It isn't reasonable."

I said, "No, that can't be. It just doesn't make any sense. It isn't reasonable."

I said, "May I go to your auditors and get them to examine it and give you a statement on it?"

He said that I could. The auditors approved the plan and wrote to the treasurer showing that the cash outlay would be reduced by a sizable sum. The treasurer said, "They must be right, but before acting we should have the approval of the auditors of the XYZ Stores Company." They approved the plan and the treasurer said, "We'll have to go and see Mr. Brown now." So we went in to explain it to Mr. Brown, who said, "No, no. You pay a higher premium in order to have a lower cash outlay? It doesn't make sense."

The treasurer said, "We've got these two letters that say we can do it. I wish you would read them."

Mr. Brown read the letters and said, "Okay, I guess we'll have to do it."

In changing the policies from the low premium to the high, the companies paid a commission on the difference, and the amount of my commission was twice as much as it would have been if I had placed the original insurance. In other words, I got the same commission that I would have been paid if I had sold $5,200,000 at the start. Then I learned that Mr. Brown had said to the original agents, "Now listen, boys. This is a good deal for you. I have a friend in the insurance business and I want you to give him half of the commission." So they did. But he didn't say that to me, because I had something to give his company that no one else had. I had a cash-saving idea. Because I worked harder and dug deeper, I didn't have to divide the commission.

I tell this story because it is an illustration of the value of digging. I dug into the minutes of the company. I dug into the corporation's resolutions. I dug all the way through because I knew if I could find a way that produced a lower cash outlay, I would have something of great value. So I dug, and dug, and dug, until I found it. Whatsoever you do, do with your might! Give it everything you've got!

One of the things we use in selling is to try to make the evidence so overwhelming that the prospect can't do anything except what you want him to do. Our men don't ask, "What's the least I have to do to get this man to say yes?" Instead, we build up, and build up, and build up, until finally the case is so overwhelming that the prospect can't do anything except say yes.

    Shortly after I moved to New York I met a Frenchman, whom I shall call Later. He and his brother owned a corporation in New York City, two corporations in Europe , and another in India. I prepared some plans for him which resulted in his buying $1,500,000 of insurance issued in one policy by Metropolitan Life. Arthur Brisbane, who at that time was a well-known columnist, wrote that it was the largest single policy ever written, and that story was printed in every metropolitan daily newspaper in the country.

    A year later Mr. Latrec called me and said, "My brother Jacques is here and I want you to prepare plans for his estate." Jacques was a citizen of France, had income from the business in Paris, received large dividends from New York, around $50,000 a year in dividends from London, and had recently married a Romanian princess. He lived in Romania and he had a home in Spain in which he spent quite a bit of time. Therefore, at his death he would have to pay inheritance taxes in France, Spain, Rumania, and the United States, and England. Also, he was paying income taxes to the United States, income taxes to Great Britain, and income taxes to France. After some deep study and after conferring with several attorneys, I advised him to create two corporations in Panama and transfer his stock in all the corporations I mentioned above to one of the Panama corporations. The result was that he paid income taxes in only one country and was subject to inheritance tax in only one country, which I think is fair and proper. All of this was done legally and, of course, was approved by his own attorneys.

The corporations were arranged so that directors' meetings could be held in any country anywhere in the world at any time, and he could dissolve them at any time.

Shortly afterwards, the second World War came along and he was in Paris all the time that it was occupied by the Germans. The plan worked out perfectly. Jacques is now dead. When he died, the inheritance tax was collected by only one country.

Some time later, the first brother, Mr. Latrec, called me and said, "Clinton, I've asked my friend Mr. Andre to see you to set up a corporation for him as you did for my brother Jacques."

Mr. Andre called me more than a month later and said his New York attorneys (a rather famous firm in New York which also had offices in Paris) told him that there was no use in seeing me because what he wanted couldn't be one, and that's why he hadn't called me either. He then arranged for a conference in his attorney's office.

Three members of the law firm were present and the tax expert opened the meeting by saying: "Mr. Davidson, when Mr. Andre transfers the securities to the Panama corporation, the income will still be income from within the United States and subject to its tax laws."

I said, "That's right."

He said, "Well, how do you plan then to change it?"

"By using two Panama corporations."

"Ah," he said, "but when the income goes from one corporation to the other in the form of dividends, it is still United States income and is still taxable in the United States."

I said, "Yes, that's right."

He said, "Well, how did you plan then to change it?"

"We didn't plan to have dividends go from one company to another," I replied.

"How then," he asked, "would you get the income from one company to the other?"

"Through bond interest."

He said, "You mean then that the bond interest does not remain American income after reaching the second corporation?"

"That's right," I said.

The tax expert turned to one of his law books and started reading. Finally the senior lawyer said, "Frank, what about it?"

He said, "I think he's right. I don't know for sure, but I think it may work. Give me a little more time."

He then turned to some other places in his books and at last said, "Yes, he's right. It will work if it flows from one corporation to the other by interest instead of by dividends." I knew it would work because it worked fro Mr. Latrec's brother.

Why was interest treated differently from dividends? I don't know. The tax law was written that way at that time; that's all

I can say. But the way to accomplish the desired results could not be found by examining the surface. One had to really work *diligently* to find the answer.

Two brothers became clients of ours and in examining their papers we learned that they had created what might be called cross trusts, or reciprocal trusts. Brother Tom transferred $5,000,000 to a trust from which all of the income went to his brother Fred. Upon Fred's death, the principal would pass to Fred's children. Fred then transferred $5,000,000 of his securities to a trust, all the income to go to Tom, and when Tom died it was intended that the principal would pass to Tom's children. After creating the trusts, each one would pass to Tom's children. After creating the trusts, each one would have the same amount of principal. We never recommended this plan because we thought that the Supreme Court would upset it. It did just that and those who used it received no benefits whatsoever from it.

I was sitting in the office leaning back in a chair against the wall, reading through the second trust document, and while reading it, I suddenly leaned forward and said, "No, no! That can't be!" I read it again and then went to our lawyer, explained it and said, "Look, George, read this. Tell me I'm wrong."

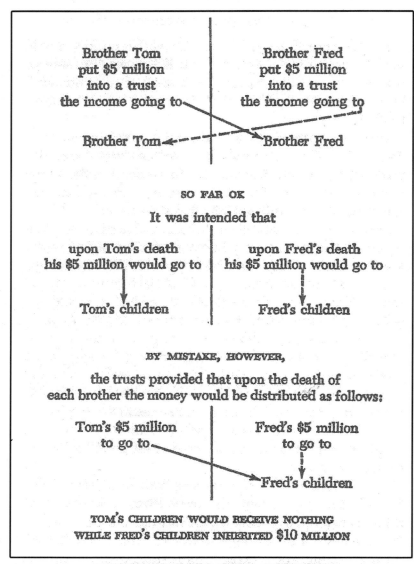

A TRUE TALE OF TWO BROTHERS

He read it and said, "That's awful. It's terrible."

Here is what had happened. From Tom's trust the income was to go to Fred, and upon Fred's death, the principal to go to Fred's children. But from Fred's death, the principal to go to Fred's children. But from Fred's trust, the cinema was to go to his brother, and upon his death, the principal would go to *his own* children. Fred's children would therefore get $10,000,000 and Tom's children would get nothing! And these trusts could not be amended, revoked, or terminated. It appeared that Tom's children would be cheated out of $5,000,000 while Fred's children got $10,000,000 (See chart on page 36.)

After George and I had studied the situation for several days, we developed a plan which we thought would correct it. I then called on the vice president in charge of the trust department of the bank that was trustee of the trusts. This bank was the largest bank in the United States at that time. After reading the paragraphs I had marked, he said, "Oh, no! I signed those trusts! I was supposed to examine them before they were put into effect! Oh, that can't be, Clinton! That can't be!" Then he said, "Have you talked to the two brothers?"

I said, "No, their attorney is over in Paris. I thought I should wait until the attorney gets back to talk to him about this. I will tell him the method we think will correct the situation, and he can tell the brothers about it if he so desires."

He added, "The attorney went over to Paris because he was threatened with a nervous breakdown."

Now, how did it happen that I discovered this error the first time I read it while the attorneys and the vice president in charge of the entire trust department of the bank read it without catching it?

Am I a better lawyer than they were? No! Do I have better brains? Absolutely not! It wasn't a matter of intellectual ability. It was a matter of thoroughness.

If you will be as thorough as the Bible advises you to be, you'll get ahead; nothing can keep you back. If, in whatever you do, you give everything you have, no one can stop you.

One thing you must be diligent in acquiring if you would get others to do what you want them to do is an understanding of the basic principles of human nature. The next chapter tells you what I learned from the Bible about that.

~ CHAPTER 3 ~

UNDERSTANDING HUMAN NATURE

ONE DAY I was talking with Marshall Field in his New York office. Although I was selling life insurance, I had never mentioned insurance to Mr. Field. His secretary came to the door and said, "Mr. Field, Mr. Smith is here to see you."

Mr. Field said, "Tell him I'll see him in a few minutes." Taking my cue, I got up to leave, but just before walking out, I said in substance, "By the way, Mr. Field, I have been wanting to mention an idea to you. There is something that you can do for your two children that they can never do for themselves. If you transfer certain securities to a trust and the trustee buys life insurance on the lives of your children, the income of that trust will be taxed only 30 per cent, whereas you are now paying 90 per cent tax on the same income. So, by following this procedure, there is a tax saving of 60 per cent of the income. Then, when the children die, the money from the insurance will come into the trust free from inheritance tax and estate tax."

Seeing that I had his interest, I continued: "I thought it would be a good idea for you to create two insurance trusts to buy a million dollars of insurance on the life of your son and a million dollars of insurance on the life of your son and a million on your daughter." All this time I was standing up and the proposal took less than five minutes.

Mr. Field said, "I think that's a good idea. Talk it over with my attorney and if he approves of it, we will do it."

I had already talked it over with the attorney and he had approved it. So in less than five minutes I made a sale of two million dollars of life insurance on which I received an immediate commission of $20,000.00 and additional commissions of $2,000.00 a year for nine years or a total of $38,000.00 As you read this true story, keep in mind that the man who sold those two policies from which he received commissions in the amount of $38,000.00 was the same man who some years before was making only $35.00 a month.

What made the difference?

I learned from the Bible that in leading a person up the four mental steps outlined in Chapter One, it is necessary to do the following things. (1) You must know everything possible about your business, your product, or the idea you are trying to get across. We went into that in the last chapter. (2) You must develop within yourself certain qualities essential to success. I am going to talk about these in future chapters. (3) You must understand human nature, know why people do what they do, and be able to cash in on that knowledge. This third factor is the subject of this chapter.

Obviously, in the less than five minutes that I spent with Marshall Field, I used all three principles. I was applying certain qualities that had been developed within myself over a period of fifty-two years, I was applying the knowledge of the life insurance business that I had acquired over twenty eight years, and I used the knowledge that I had of human nature.

Now let me tell you about another sale which I tried to make, and failed, because I failed to apply all of these principles. This happened less than five years before I sold Mr. Field the two million dollars' worth of life insurance. A general agent said to me, "Clinton, I can get you an interview with John Lawrence, if you would like to try to sell him."

Now, Mr. Lawrence was a very prominent, wealthy man, so I replied, "I certainly would like it."

The general agent called me later and said, "I can't get the interview with Mr. Lawrence yet, but if you will see his secretary she will give you all the information you need, and after you prepare a report you can then see Mr. Lawrence." I saw his secretary, and she gave me the information I requested. I studied the information, prepared a written report, and got an appointment with Mr. Lawrence.

His office was in a building on Park Avenue. When I entered it I was amazed to find a wood-burning fireplace in his office. This was unusual for a New York City office. Around the room I saw many other things that indicated that Mr. Lawrence was an unusual man in many respects. When I had completed my report, he said, "Well, you haven't analyzed my ambitions correctly."

I said, "Well, how about your plantation and the plan I have for it?"

He replied, "I'd rather not think about that today."

I made some further effort to sell him, but all he would say was, "I'll study your report."

I lost out on that sale because of one mistake that I made. I was short on number 3. I just didn't size Mr. Lawrence up correctly, and I didn't treat him the way he should have been treated. I didn't have a picture of Mr. Lawrence in my mind when I wrote that report. I had a correct picture of his properties, but not of his personality - not of Mr. Lawrence himself.

An idea is like a coiled spring; it has its own motive power and when you put that idea in someone's mind it begins to uncoil and go to work. So, after leaving Mr. Lawrence, I said to myself, "I put some ideas in his mind which are bound to work, and I just know he is going to buy at least a million dollars' worth of life insurance. I know he will!"

A month or two later, the general agent called me up and said, "Mr. Lawrence phoned me. He told me that he has a friend who does not work in life insurance, but who has a license to sell life insurance, and he wants this friend to get the commission from a million dollars' worth of life insurance to be placed on Mr. Lawrence's life. He also said that Mr. Davidson is not to get any part of this, because Mr. Davidson didn't give him any of the ideas that resulted in his buying this life insurance."

The general agent continued, "Mr. Lawrence said, "These ideas are my own. I am buying this insurance because of my ideas and not because of any ideas that Davidson gave me.'"

I fell down completely on one point. I may have prepared a good estate plan; I may have used some of the principles of selling correctly, but I misjudged Mr. Lawrence, and therefore I lost the sale.

After many years of study and experience, I am convinced that the Bible is the best textbook for understanding human nature. I once made a decision which was an important turning point in my life because of what the Bible had taught me about people.

While I worked in Buffalo, New York, I learned that the life insurance company I represented had a vacancy in one of its general agencies in New York City. In those days general agencies were greatly sought after, and from a money-making viewpoint, New York City was considered the greatest prize of all.

I wanted that agency, and I called on the vice president at the home office and made application for it. Now, moving from a very small agency in Buffalo to New York seemed quite a step to the vice president, who quite properly doubted my ability to handle the situation. "Have you ever worked in New York?" he asked.

"No," I had to admit.

"Well," explained the vice president, "in this New York agency your business would come largely from very wealthy men who are 'tough nuts to crack.' I am afraid that with your meagre experience in Louisville and Buffalo, you would not be able to sell the type of prospect you would find in New York."

I was a timid, backward young man at the time, and I hesitated to express my opinion, especially to the vice president of my company. But I had learned that no matter what else I might question there was never any need to question what I read in the Bible. So I replied with complete confidence:

"Mr. Smith, I have just finished reading the Book of Exodus, which tells in detail the story of the journeys of the children of Israel for forty years. As I read it, I was astounded to observe that those people, some three or four thousand years ago, reacted in every particular just exactly as the people I know in Kentucky and in Buffalo would react today under similar conditions. This book has proved to me that human nature is the same the world over and that it has not changed within the past four thousand years. Now, if those people I know in Kentucky would react today, I am not afraid of the difference I may find between the people in New York City and the people in Louisville or Buffalo."

This reasoning was not powerful enough to convince the vice president, and I did not get the agency. But later on when I did come to New York City as an independent life insurance broker, I quickly proved that what I had said was true. The second year I was in New York City I wrote and delivered more insurance business (on the basis of new premiums) than the entire New York City general agency which I had hoped to take over. Not only that, but I personally did more business than the combined volume of both the agency which I left behind and the agency I had hoped to get in New York.

This may sound boastful but only by presenting my actual results can I demonstrate that what I told that vice president was correct: the principles of human nature governing people in Louisville were the same governing people in the great metropolis. Or, to say it in another way, what I had learned about human nature and salesmanship through a careful study of the Bible gave me a foundation that enabled me to do better in New York City than men who had been there for years.

Most of what I know about human nature I have learned from the Bible and from my personal experience in dealing with human beings. The Bible provides an amazingly accurate and detailed history of man for thousands of years, and the Bible's description of its characters is unbiased. Bad qualities are given just as much weight as good qualities. For example, the Apostle Peter had weaknesses that are reported in as much detail as his strengths. King David is referred to as a man after God's own heart, but his wrongdoings are not omitted from the record and no excuses for them are given. In other literature, we sometimes find the life of an outstanding character reported by both an enemy and by a friend, and in reading the two reports it is difficult to realize that the writers are describing the same man. You can't learn much about human nature from that kind of material. To learn the fundamentals of human nature and to understand human motivations, frailties, and strengths, all reported accurately and without bias from life, read the Bible.

Let me tell you how an understanding of human nature enabled my associate and myself to sell a prospect who was inclined to take the opposite side on practically every subject that could be brought up. My associate, Raymond Hartz, and I had luncheon with this prospect some years ago. He had formed the habit of taking the contrary side of every subject, largely for the purpose of testing the validity of the ideas that were presented to him. During luncheon we mentioned the desirability of using a certain type of trust which had been planned by our organization. Although the prospect did not practice law, he had graduated from law school and he had made a fair study of taxation. He immediately began trying to punch holes in our plan, and continued doing so until 8:00 PM when we parted. We met again at 9:30 the next morning and he still continued trying to find weak spots in the plan. The time finally arrived, however, when he admitted that the trust plan was entirely satisfactory. When our second suggestion was made, the same procedure was followed, and this continued on for ten days. At one point our prospect mentioned that he did not carry much life insurance and that he had never thought very favorably about doing so. At the close of the tenth day he said, "You have not said a word about what you get out of this. Suppose we discuss that tomorrow morning."

Mr. Hartz and I discussed the subject that night. After ten days of having our recommendations continuously objected to, we thought it might be helpful to let our prospect object to something that would be helpful to let our prospect object to something that would turn out to be helpful to us. Mr. Hartz suggested it might be desirable that we begin the conversation the next morning as follows. Our compensation, we would say, usually consisted of commissions on insurance purchased for the purpose of having sufficient cash funds on hand to pay the estate taxes, but as our friend was opposed to life insurance, we would skip that subject and work out some other plan.

We did this and he immediately took the other side, saying, "But I have not been opposed to life insurance, and if that is the usual basis, I would like very much to hear what it is." We then explained that the amount of life insurance he needed was $1,200,000, but that he would probably think the amount was too large. He replied that he could not decide whether it was too large or too small until he had complete information. During that same day, he signed an application for $1,200,000 of life insurance, made a prepayment on the premium, and was examined and accepted. This was a case where being able to judge human nature correctly was of the utmost importance.

Elmer Wheeler in *The American Salesman* suggests five things to say for better relations with one's fellow beings. They are -

1. "I am proud of you!" The five best words to make people feel good. Try them on the boss, employee, wife, husband, friend. Elevate their ego, and they'll never let you down.

2. "What is your opinion?" The four greatest words to gain willing information from the toughest person or utter stranger. Compliment people's judgement: they like that.

3. "If you please!" Three magic words to get fast action out of people for the things and favors you ask of them. Add them to your requests.

4. "Thank you!" Two words to make people *glad* they did a favor. Never fail to use them. "Thank you" is an important expression in every language.

5. "You!" The one word to make the most friends. People like to hear about *themselves*. So use "you" instead of "I" - the smallest word in the world.

All these expressions seem to come naturally when you practice the admonition Moses gave 3500 years ago: "Thou shalt love they neighbor as thyself" (Leviticus 19:18). That is they key that unlocks the deepest secrets of human nature.

~ CHAPTER 4 ~

GETTING PEOPLE TO BELIEVE YOU

A FRIEND ASKED me what I had to do to get a man to part with a check for a million dollars or more. Handing over the check is, of course, the conclusion of the four mental steps outlined in Chapter One for getting people to do what you want. When the fourth step - action - involves a million dollars, it is a mighty satisfactory conclusion!

"You must know," I answered, "that I have to do many things to get a check for a million dollars. But if you are asking me to single out the most important factor of all in persuading a man to turn loose that much money, my answer is this: *Get his confidence.* Get him to believe you 100 percent."

A ten-dollar bill states:

**FEDERAL RESERVE NOTE
THE UNITED STATES OF AMERICA
WILL PAY TO THE BEARER ON DEMAND
TEN DOLLARS**

A one-dollar bill states:

**SILVER CERTIFICATE
THIS CERTIFIES THAT THERE IS
ON DEPOSIT IN THE TREASURY OF
THE UNITED STATES OF AMERICA
ONE DOLLAR
IN SILVER PAYABLE
TO THE BEARER ON DEMAND**

Behind each one-dollar bill there is a silver dollar, but behind the ten-dollar bill only because merchants have confidence in the notes (promises to pay) of the United States. The ten-dollar bill is money solely because people have confidence in the United States. There is no "hard" money behind it.

It is true that a man had to have a lot of confidence in me to give a check for $1,000,000 in exchange for some insurance policy, but he had to have even more confidence to appoint the company I organized, Fiduciary Counsel, Inc., to supervise his investments. When we employed a new representative, I said to him:

"Jack, if a life insurance man sold someone $5,000,000 of life insurance, he would be jumping up and down with enthusiasm and would probably say, 'Just think of the confidence that man placed in me.' The annual premium would probably be about $200,000, so the insurance buyer would be actually committing himself to not more than $200,000. If a bond salesman sold an individual $1,000,000 of bonds of a new issue, he also would be extremely enthusiastic and would be greatly complimented by the purchaser's confidence. The amount of this investment would be five times that of the insurance investment just mentioned. On the other hand, when you persuade a man who is worth $10,000,000 to employ Fiduciary Counsel, Inc. to supervise all of his investments, he must have ten times as much confidence as he had in buying $1,000,000 of bonds and fifty times as much confidence as he had in buying $5,000,000 of life insurance. Just remember, Jack, that when he signs the contract letter employing Fiduciary Counsel, he is trusting us with everything that he has. Therefore, confidence in us is of the utmost importance, and before we can secure him as a client we must do everything to build confidence in us to the *nth* degree."

How is such confidence built? It is an intangible, elusive sort of process, hard to put into words. However, I would say it requires the following conditions:

First of all, *to build confidence you must "know your stuff."* The better you know what you are talking about, the quicker you can persuade the other person to trust you.

Second, *you must avoid all exaggeration.* But not only must you never exaggerate; also, *you must practice the art of understatement rigorously and consciously,* almost to a point so extreme that the typical salesman would label it ridiculous!

Third, *you must be willing and able to prove your case with facts developed from several different angles.*

Fourth, you must present your case in a tone of quiet authority, without apology or uncertainty, but without arrogance or bombast either.

Just as water rises no higher that itself, so the confidence of others in you will never be greater than the confidence you have in yourself. Confidence in one's self is imperative and yet nothing is more irritating to others than egotism. We must try to seek the assurance which exists between the extremes of egotism and inferiority.

Some years ago I was puzzled as to how one could have supreme confidence and yet not be egotistical. I found it in the New Testament. The Apostle Paul said, "I can do all things." That expressed supreme confidence, but if he had stopped there it would also indicate egotism. He did not stop there, however. The full sentence is, "I can do all things through Christ which strengtheneth me" (Philippians 4:13). The man who believes this has calm, quiet confidence, but because his confidence is based upon God's power and not his own power, there is never the slightest speck of egotism. Those who believe the Twenty-third Psalm, or the promise, "My God shall supply all your need according to his riches in glory by Christ Jesus," will never lack confidence and never be egotistical.

Fifth, *you must use concrete words and phrases.* You must be specific and explicit. Your proposals must be defined and delimited with the utmost precision.

Sixth, *you must know all the weak points in your proportion and present them to your prospect along with the strong points* so that the other fellow has as complete and true a picture of the proposal as you have. This procedure may seem strange, but it strengthens your hand immeasurably in the tight places. It keeps you from fears that the prospect will unexpectedly find one of your hidden loopholes or soft spots. It gives you the power of truth.

Here is how I used it. In placing million-dollar policies on the lives of men over fifty-five, it often seemed just as difficult to get the policies issued by the insurance companies as to make the sales. I developed the habit of sending in with the application a complete report, and I always pointed out every unfavorable fact which I had been able to determine. If the man had had some serious disease many years before, I investigated it thoroughly and reported all of the facts to the company. I was in a better position to report confidential information regarding a client's financial standing than the company's inspection bureau. I always explained to the applicant that he would be inspected from the viewpoint of moral habits, and asked him to tell me of any adverse information that might pop up, along with his own explanation. I had learned that many cases are turned down, not because of positive adverse information, but because the company believes it has not received full information and is afraid that some adverse information may have been withheld. My procedure enabled me to build up confidence in the companies I dealt with most frequently and these companies felt that they were always getting complete information. In fact, I was told quite often that they received more complete information on my cases than they were able to get on any others. Several times when my personal information differed from that of the company's inspection bureau, the latter accepted my information because it believed that I had better sources.

For many years, the largest life insurance company in this country did not deal with brokers. When it was announced that the company would consider doing so, the vice president told me that he was making the change with great reluctance. He said, "You brokers who handle large cases have been able to bring too much pressure to bear upon the medical department through the general agents. I want you to know that we do not care a rap about the size of a case and if you bring a $500,000 case in here, you will get no more attention than the agent who brings in a $1,000 case. Our company is set up so that the agency division can have no influence whatsoever upon the medical division."

My first case was for a policy of $1,500,000 upon the life of an internationally famous man who was a co-director with Mr.

Haley Fiske, then president of this insurance company. When I brought my client in to be examined, I was told that Mr. Fiske would like to see him. So, following the examination, I took him into Mr. Fiske's office where they chatted for quite a while. Several days later, the vice president called me and said:

"Clinton, we have had some difficulty getting a specimen of urine with the proper specific gravity. One day it is too high and the next day it is too low. Of course, this is a minor matter, but it is necessary to have a specimen within the standard limits. Your client has become a little peeved at our requests and he may refuse to provide any more specimens. We mentioned the matter to Mr. Fiske and he wondered if you would explain the matter to your client and get an additional specimen from him."

I replied, "Most certainly not. You made very clear to me that you would not permit the agency department or a broker to deal with the medical department. You said that after the applicant was brought to the doctor, everything from then on was in the hands of the medical department. My client is now in the hands of your medical department and I will have nothing to do with it until the case is either issued or declined."

Was he amazed! He couldn't believe that an agent would refuse to call on a client and request an additional specimen for a case having an annual premium in excess of $80,000. Two things happened. The policy was issued; it was the largest policy ever issued in one contract by one company up to that time. And from then on the medical department had complete confidence in me and I received wonderful co-operation from them.

Seventh, *you must present the proposition that is best for your prospect* and not the proposition that is, *sub rosa*, best for you. I do not recommend this on moral grounds alone. I recommend it also because to follow this precept will give you the courage of a lion. It will strengthen your confidence at the time when it most needs strengthening. It will make your defenses impregnable.

Eighth, *answer all questions frankly, openly, fully and without reservation.* You can do this only if you have also observed points two, five, six and seven.

Ninth (and here is one that ninety per cent of us fall down on), *all information given to you by a client or prospect must be kept strictly confidential,* and even clients' names must never be mentioned without permission to do so. Aren't you amazed at the number of security salesmen and life insurance men who constantly refer to what their customers have done? "Mr. Jones had just purchased 1,000 shares of Warner Brothers," you are told, or, "Mr. Smith bought a $100,000 policy in our company last month." One cannot be too cautious in this respect. One reason why "keeping confidence" pays is that so few can be trusted 100 per cent to do so.

Here is an illustration showing how it pays. Mr. Hartz, an associate of mine, immediately after opening an office in another city, sought the co-operation of a local bank which happened to be the fourth largest in the country. A committee of officers invited him to tell his story and, during the discussion, he mentioned that we were preparing plans for one of their directors. "Which one?" a vice president asked. "I'm sorry, but we have one rule that is never broken," Mr. Hartz replied. "Because our business is so confidential, we cannot even mention our clients' names without their specific permission. But if it's important, I shall request such permission," he added.

The vice president said that it was not necessary. Later on, he told Mr. Hartz that every officer in the room knew who the director was, as he had already told them about the work we were doing. "Our confidence in you increased several hundred per cent when you refused to divulge his name," he said. As confidence in Mr. Hartz developed, the chairman of the board became interested and called a special luncheon meeting of the board of directors, at which the entire time was given us to present an explanation of our organization's activities. Our second client in that city was secured that afternoon. Yes, he was one of the directors who attended the meeting.

Now, a special meeting of the board of directors of the fourth largest bank in the United States to hear our sales talk was quite an achievement for a young man under thirty, practically a stranger in that city. He did it by building confidence.

Through a similar circumstance, the unrestricted management of $3,500,000 in securities was obtained for another associate of mine before the client had even seen him or corresponded with him. Can you imagine granting the unrestricted right to buy, sell, and reinvest $3,500,000, to a person you had never met or corresponded with? I tell this because I believe that less than 10 per cent of us realize how important this subject is. From experience, I have learned that even bank presidents occasionally betray minor confidences.

In 1934 I did some work for a man who was worth approximately $100,000,000 - even after the depression! Shortly afterwards, I solicited his cousin, who asked for references. I was unusually anxious to secure this client because, in addition to being a most successful businessman, his reputation for fair dealing, uprightness and practical philanthropy was not exceeded by anyone in his community. I wanted to tell him that I had done work for his wealthier cousin but I could not do so because I had not asked the first client's permission, and I always avoid making such a request until all the work has been completed. However, the new client was secured in November and my work with him continued until June, and for seven months I never hinted that his cousin, whom he saw daily, was also a client.

After my work for the first client was completed, he gladly permitted me to use his name as a reference. The second client, when I told him, found it hard to believe that I had worked for his cousin for three months before I met him. By this time the second client had purchased $1,800,000 of insurance, so he knew what I had at stake when he asked for references.

This fact did more than anything else to develop his confidence in me. Later, when he sought to replace the part-time management he had been giving his investments with a full-time investment manager to whom he could give the unrestricted right to buy, sell, and reinvest, he permitted me to select this manager for him. Quite naturally, I appreciated the degree of confidence this indicated.

Tenth, *resist all intimations that you are acting in your own and not in your prospect's interest.* Such insinuations would be denied calmly, quietly, but firmly. The salesman who has had the courage to live up to the other nine requirements will have no difficulty handling the tenth.

The most harmful idea which arises in the mind of a prospect is this: the belief that all salesmen lie. (Some, to be polite, call it exaggeration or inaccuracy.) The prospect's mind, instead of accepting the salesman's statements at their face value, always has a strong contrary idea that what the salesman is saying is merely "sales talk."

This idea is so powerful a negative force that when a prospect told me that another life insurance representative claimed to have the best policy contract and the lowest cost of any company, I usually gave the answer (the true answer, by the way!): "Oh, that's just sales talk!" Believe it or not, that was almost always the only answer I ever needed to counteract the other man's claims. The exaggeration of sales talk is so universally accepted that merely to stigmatize another salesman's claims as "sales talk" often disposes of them instantly, without argument.

Assume that you are calling on a man worth $1,000,000. Before you go to see him, you know that hundreds of people have been trying to take his money away from him ever since he has had any business responsibilities. You also know that he has learned the difference between 100 per cent absolute truth and what is commonly called "sales talk." You also know that he will regard all salesmen's statements as "mere sales talk" until they are proved to be otherwise. Now suppose that instead of an ordinary run-of-the-mill salesman, you have the reputation of telling the truth under all circumstances, no matter how embarrassing it may be to you or how much it may cost you. If these facts are known to your prospect, and your truthfulness has previously been established, your job will be twice as easy.

How can you establish in your prospect's mind the conviction that you do not exaggerate, lie or misrepresent in any way, even in the smallest particular? My best counsel is, "Impress him with your veracity." To *impress* truthfulness you must *possess* it.

I know of nothing that will improve your veracity more than reading and studying the Bible. The truth is exalted, and lying denounced in at least ninety-three separate references in the Bible. I shall quote only a few:

Psalm 119:163   I hate and abhor lying.

Psalm 120:2   Deliver my soul, O Lord, from lying lips, and from a deceitful tongue.

Proverbs 6:17   (Of seven things God hates, lying is denounced twice.)

Proverbs 12:22   Lying lips are abomination to the Lord: but they that deal truly are his delight.

Proverbs 12:19   The lip of truth shall be established for ever: but a lying tongue is but for a moment.

A study of the Bible will improve your reputation for absolute truthfulness under all conditions, and this will give people confidence in whatever you say - confidence that will work for you more and more.

~ CHAPTER 5 ~

MAKING THINGS CLEAR

IN 1941 I SUCCEEDED in getting a bill enacted by Congress which resulted in the government's paying to business corporations a total of five billion dollars. My son, who had devised the plan, was helping me on it, but I received very little help from others. It was difficult during the days of President Franklin D. Roosevelt to get a bill enacted that would pay General Motors approximately $45,000,000 (and that is exactly what it did), because in the eyes of Mr. Roosevelt that one time was enough to condemn it!

The subject was rather complicated and I was invited by a group composed of Democratic members of the Ways and Means Committee of Congress to explain the bill to them. The man who arranged the meeting, Congressman Wesley Disney of Tulsa, Oklahoma, said after the meeting, "Clinton, how in the world did you ever learn to explain everything so clearly? I have watched you in various places, and not matter what group you are talking to, everybody present appears to understand you perfectly."

Making things clear is of the utmost importance in getting your prospect interested in what you are trying to put across. Inability to clarify often results in failure to get the action you want.

I replied to Congressman Disney, "That's the simplest thing in the world, Wes. I learned that from Jesus."

When I was a young man I made a study of how Jesus did His teaching. I read the Gospels of Matthew, Mark, Luke and John. I found that Christ used the same method over and over. He always referred to something with which the person to whom He was talking was very familiar.

To the farmer He said, "You know about sowing seeds, don't you?"

The farmer said, "Huh, do I! How many times I've gotten up at daylight and walked over the rough ground until dark sowing seeds! And when I was through with the day's work, I hardly had enough strength to get to bed. Do I know about sowing!"

"Well," Jesus said, "the Kingdom of Heaven is just like that."

He said to the housewife, "You know about baking bread, don't you? You know how to use leaven to make the bread rise."

"Do I!" she exclaimed.

"Well," said Jesus, "the Kingdom of Heaven is just like that."

He said to the gem merchant, "You know what it means to have the brightest, most lustrous, biggest pearl of all, don't you?"

"The Kingdom of Heaven," Jesus explained, "is just like that. It's the most important thing in the world."

That's how Jesus made things clear. And that's all there is to it. The great things that come from God are so simple. Try Jesus' method. When you have to explain something to another person, ask yourself, "What is it this person is most familiar with? What is it he understands inside and out and knows all about?" The answer to that question will give you the key you need.

Here is how I used this method to sell insurance. In my early days of selling, when I was working for the John Hancock Mutual Life Insurance Company, I called at the home of a man who, I had been told, was going to buy $1,000 worth of life insurance. After listening to my sales story he said, "I want to buy a thousand dollars' insurance, but your company's rate is too high. I've been talking to the Verity Insurance people, and their rate is 20 per cent lower."

I replied, "Yes, you are right. Their rates are about 20 per cent lower." Then I added, "By the way, I notice that you have a sectional bookcase here with glass doors on it. You know, you can buy a sectional bookcase without glass doors and it will be about 20 per cent cheaper. I wonder why you paid the extra 20 per cent."

"Oh," he said, "they keep out the dust. They preserve the books, and it is well worth the 20 per cent additional cost."

"Well," I said, "I didn't know. I thought maybe you were one of those who think that price is the only thing that counts... all you looked for was to get the lowest price and nothing else mattered, and that's why I wondered about the bookcase. Now," I said, "let me show you *why* this policy costs 20 per cent more."

When I finished my explanation, my client was convinced that life insurance is just like any other commodity: the customer usually gets what he pays for - just that and nothing more.

One thing I learned from the teaching methods of Jesus was the importance of *picturing* what you are trying to get across in terms of what your prospect understands. A Chinese proverb states, "One picture is worth a thousand words." That may be literally true if one is speaking Chinese, and especially if he is trying to speak that language to someone who doesn't understand it!

But I think the literal application of this picture idea is entirely overdone. I have never seen a picture made by brush or pen that could sell a million-dollar life insurance policy! However, I have sold a good many million-dollar policies by painting pictures on the minds of my prospects. And I have found that those pictures had to be simple and clear. I used to keep on my desk a framed motto which read, "Keep it *big* and it will dominate. Keep it *simple* and it will be understood." When we got into the business of Estate Planning, there was a tendency for the proposals to become quite complicated. One of the things I had to do constantly was to take the material that came from the lawyers, which was often too complicated for our prospects to grasp easily, and to put it into terms they could *see* - simply and clearly.

It is no easy matter to get any man to write out a check for $1,000,000, especially if he receives in return only a contract which he has not read. Usually he does not read it, because he thinks he will not understand all of it. In such cases, it is not only necessary for the purchaser to have absolute confidence in the truthfulness of your statements but also it is necessary in presenting these ideas to use *vivid* language. Your words must not only paint pictures but paint them *deeply*, in vivid colors.

When I first stared selling, I knew nothing about vividness of expression and I had not learned how to develop it. I heard a psychology professor say that one of the most striking demonstrations of vividness of expression was to be found in Kipling's *Jungle Book*, especially where the wolf family found the little Man Child. While the professor was telling me of Kipling's talent for vividness, I was asking myself: "What stories told me during childhood remain most vividly in my mind?" The answer was not difficult to find. I immediately remembered that as a child of five or six years my mother used to hold me on her lap in front of the grate fire and read to me from a book of Bible stories. Daniel in the lion's den, the fall of Jericho, Abraham's willingness to offer his son as a sacrifice - all these stories are pictured vividly in my memory to this day.

Let me quote you a few sentences from the sixth chapter of Daniel as an example of the vivid description to be found in that book:

Then the king commanded, and they bought Daniel, and cast him into the den of lions. Now the king spake and said unto Daniel, Thy God whom thou serves continually, he will deliver thee. And a stone was brought, and laid upon the mouth of the den; and the king sealed it with his own signet, and with the signet of his lords; that the purpose might not be changed concerning Daniel.

Then the king went to his palace, and passed the night fasting neither were instruments of music brought before him: and his sleep went from him. Then the king arose very early in the morning, and went in haste unto the den of lions. And when he came to the den, he cried with a lamentable voice unto Daniel: and the king spake and said to Daniel, O Daniel, servant of the living God, is they God, whom thou servest continually, able to deliver thee from the lions? Then said Daniel unto the king, O king, live for ever. My God hath sent his angel, and hath shut the lions' mouths, that they have not hurt me (Daniel 6:16-22).

As a child I pictured an angel, holding shut the massive jaws of a hungry lion, and this whole episode was very real to me from hearing this story read from the Bible. Read the story aloud and notice how much meaning each word conveys.

The entire first six chapters of Daniel are excellent examples of vivid expression. They tell of Nebuchadnezzar's dream, the "fiery furnace," and "the handwriting on the wall." Read them! The whole Bible is full of marvelous examples of vividness of expression: "The fathers have eaten a sour grape, and the children's teeth are set on edge" (Jeremiah 31:29). How much more vivid than saying: "The sons are being punished for their father's sins."

Kipling wrote of his snake saying: "Kaa seemed to pour himself along the ground." Can you imagine any more picturesque way of describing the muscular forward movement of a snake?

"His foot broke the coffee-colored ice that filled a frozen wheel track." How much that sentence tells, and how vividly.

I have frequently observed that strong, powerful verbs add much to the vividness of a sentence. John Van Dyke in his "The Dawn in Temperate Climates" uses verbs to splendid advantage to gain vividness. Just note them in this paragraph:

The shafts of light are *shot up, reflected, bent, thrown back*. They *strike* the clouds; the darkness *lifts* into space; the mists *stir*, the light *spreads* and *falls*, the hue *creeps* down; the color of the rose *lifts* to a high pitch, the poplar *shakes* night from its leaves....

The verb is a natural picture-maker; it is quick to give us a sense of life and activity. Therefore, the vivid verb is one of the best tools of the writer or speaker who would achieve sure control of vivid phrases. It is a fact that verbs are far more effective than adjectives for producing action. Adjectives paint pretty pictures, but verbs move.

An oil furnace manufacturer put out a booklet to dissatisfy the owners of old-fashioned oil burners with their equipment so that they might be made to purchase the new and improved equipment which he was selling. I have never seen a better example of vividness of language used commercially.

The visitor's every sense *shouted* out to him that the Parsons family *owned* one of these old-fashioned horse-and-buggy oil burners. Your nose *knew* it by the half-musty, half-acrid smell of fuel oil in the air, an odor that *became* so strong at times that you literally *tasted* it under your tongue. Your ears *seized* upon the fact from the hoarse roaring that *came* intermittently up from the basement. Your eyes *informed* you that the burner *leaked*, for the fine rugs *were traced* with oil spots *tracked* up from a dripping basement floor. And even had one *been blind* and *deaf* and *had a cold* in the head, the slimy film of oil mist that *covered* the smooth and polished arms of the chairs would have *announced* the sad news by way of the finger tips.

In 1938, at the request of Frank Phillips, then Chairman of the Board of Phillips Petroleum Corporation, I succeeded in getting a change in the Federal tax law. Mr. Phillips also asked one of his vice presidents, Will Davis, to assist me. Mr. Phillips, strange to say, was opposed to a college education, and had talked with me at length on this subject. When he introduced Mr. Davis to me, he said, "Will is an excellent writer and, although I object to a college education in general, I must say that Will is a good man in spite of it."

Mr. Davis replied: "Uncle Frank, you are mistaken. I was not fortunate enough to attend college."

Mr. Phillips said in surprise, "How is it you are such a good writer if you didn't go to college?"

"When I was a young boy, my mother called in all the children of the neighborhood for a short time every afternoon, except Sunday, and we read the Bible. That went on for a good many years and, although I did not know it at the time, I was studying English from the best textbook that exists."

Will Davis was right, and no one knows it better than John L. Lewis. When he gets wrought up and is determined to put his ideas across, many of his most vivid phrases are taken directly from the Bible.

If you can make things clear, you will find it much easier to get the favorable attention of the person with whom you are dealing, and to lead his mind up the four steps to a favorable decision. When it comes to the last step, however, serious obstacles usually arise before your prospect is ready to take the action you want. Handling these obstacles is what I want to take up next.

~ CHAPTER 6 ~

HOW TO HANDLE OBSTACLES

ONE OF THE MOST important things to know is how to handle obstacles. They can be turned into steppingstones to success! The person who knows and believes the promises of God is in a better position to do this than anyone else. The Bible says, "All things work together for good to them that love God" (Romans 8:28).

There are two central ideas in the Bible. One is that God is all-powerful. The other is that He loves us just as much as a man loves his own children. Now, if God is all-powerful and loves us that much, what do we have to worry about? All things work together for our good - even the things that we can't understand! Ponder that word "together." If you expect everything to lead you to your immediate goal, you will be disappointed. But if life's experiences mean anything, they teach that we can profit from trouble and heartbreak. We may not see the cosmic pattern at the time, but when we look back, we can usually see that many things *have* worked together for our good. "God moves in a mysterious way his wonders to perform." Those words by William Cowper are literally true.

The process is something like baking a cake. Suppose you taste each ingredient in the recipe separately. Take a pinch of flour and taste it. Is it good? Certainly not! Neither is baking powder! or salt, or shortening! But - *put them together* and bake them according to the recipe, and you have a result that makes you want more. Just so, a man has to trust his God that the events which look gloomy are going to turn out all right.

One of the greatest ambitions of Saint Paul was to preach the gospel of Christ in Rome. But he had no money, it seemed impossible for him to get to Rome. Then came his imprisonment. That certainly was not a pleasant experience. He was thrown into jail and held there for two years. Who could enjoy an experience like that?

Yet what was the end result? At the end of two years, exercising his right as a Roman citizen, Paul appealed to Caesar, and the law of Rome compelled the authorities to send him to Rome as a prisoner to be tried in the imperial court. Paul was a prisoner, yes; but he was a prisoner with the privilege of preaching to the imperial guard as well as to never have seen Rome. All things work together for good to those who love the Lord.

A salesman was selling a set of books to a young businessman at his home. He had shown his samples and told the story of how the books would benefit the prospect, and had actually reached the place where he was filling out the order. Then the young prospect's mother-in-law came sailing into the room. Her jaw was firm.

"John," she began in a withering tone, "have you bought some more books?"

John faltered, "Why, er-, ah-, no, Mother."

Here was a hurdle the book agent had not foreseen. He had to think fast and do something promptly, or that order was gone.

That was as clear as day. Disdainfully folding up his samples, picking up his prospectus and the half-filled-out order blank, he got up as if to leave. He said, "Mr. Brown, if your mother-in-law will not let you buy this set of books, there is no use wasting any more time!"

The young man reddened at the inference. "Nobody is going to say what I do about these books!" said John. "Give me that oder blank. I'm going to take them!"

The agent won - by quick thinking, quick acting, and saying the right thing at exactly the right time. He had turned what could easily have been a costly circumstance into a means for compelling the young prospect to take the books. He had quickly capitalized on a serious obstacle, and had converted it into an order.

Let's take another example. One of my associates and I had succeeded in getting a wealthy man to apply for $2,000,000 in life insurance. No one had ever sold him insurance before and our success had come only after long and arduous efforts. Imagine our disappointment, therefore, when after applying to every company in the United States and Canada, we found that we could get a total of only $1,300,000 on this man's life. The potential commissions on the other $700,000 that we could not get amounted to more than $20,000. I decided not to mourn over it, however, remembering the many times I had proved the truth of the Bible promise, "All things work together for good to them that love God."

When we delivered the policies and informed the man that our most urgent efforts had secured only $1,300,000, his whole attitude about insurance suddenly changed. He had been thinking that insurance was easy to get. Every day, literally, one or more insurance men came to see his secretary begging for the chance to see him and sell him insurance. Now, when after all these years he had finally capitulated and agreed to buy, he couldn't buy what he had the money to pay for. That was a new angle to this very wealthy man who was accustomed to getting what he wanted.

We saw a chance to capitalize on that change of viewpoint. Our client had three sons. "Why wait to insure them until something happens to make them uninsurable?" we asked. "Why not protect them now?" The idea appealed to him. The boys were examined, and each was covered for a half million dollars. The result: a million and a half of insurance we might never had the first application of the father been accepted and written without difficulty.

The event which we felt like mourning about had been turned into a distinct asset for us. But that was not the end of our good fortune resulting from what first seemed to be a misfortune. When we found that we were unable to get the full $2,000,000 applied for in the first instance, we did not cease our search. The $1,300,000 policy had been delivered and paid for. But we kept looking for someone who would insure this man in the amount that he desired. Finally, we found that we could get him $2,200,000 of single premium insurance, he accepted it, notwithstanding the fact that he already had bought the first large policy.

In other words, instead of selling only $2,000,000, which had been the very top of our original hopes, we had sold this man and his family $5,000,000! This sort of thing has happened to me so many times that now whenever a serious obstacle arises, I always ask the question, "How can this be turned into a steppingstone?"

Perhaps the best illustration in existence of profiting from difficulties is the story of Joseph, told in the Book of Genesis, chapters 37-50. Joseph's brothers threw him into a deep pit where he might have perished. This obstacle became the first step to the throne of Egypt. He was sold as a slave to a caravan. This second obstacle resulted in putting him in the house of the captain of Pharaoh's guard. He was then falsely accused of attempted sexual assault and thrown into prison. This third obstacle brought him in contact with one who would later introduce him to the Pharaoh, which led to his becoming the executive ruler of the greatest nation in the world at that time - ruling directly under Pharaoh. Each obstacle proved to be an important step in his rise to this position of great power and honor. God saw to it that all things worked together for Joseph's good.

About fifty years ago most residences in the large cities contained a storage house at the back of the lot. One man thought that he saw an opportunity to capitalize on this condition, and so he invented and had manufactured a large number of combination padlocks to be used on these storage houses. However, when the prospective purchasers learned that it was necessary to use a light to open the lock at night, they would not buy, and the manufacturer finally decided to sell all of them as junk metal. A friend of mine in Louisville, Kentucky, bought the entire lot at the junk metal price. He then prepared a printed circular which explained that this was the safest lock that could be obtained because it could not be opened at night *without the aid of a light*, and no burglar would dare to use a light for this purpose. He sold all of the locks at many times the price he had paid for them. He made the other man's obstacle his steppingstone to success!

Very often the obstacle which prevents the prospect from taking the initiative and saying, "I will buy it," is that of price. There are two methods usually used to eliminate this objection.

In the drawing below, the square at the left represents the value of the article in the mind of the prospect. The large drawing at the right represents the size of the price in the prospect's mind when he first hears it. The salesman must either increase the value of the article to his prospect, or reduce the size of the price in the buyer's mind.

VALUE	PRICE

In the drawing, the larger square (at the left) now represents the value of the article *which the salesman has planted in the mind of the prospect*. The salesman has increased this value in his prospect's mind by pointing out various uses and needs which were previously unknown to him. Because the value of the product, or service, is now seen as so much larger than the price, the price is no longer the controlling objection, although it remains exactly as it originally appeared int he prospect's mind.

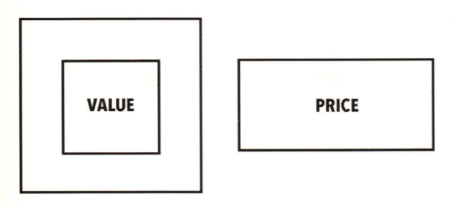

Now, in the figures below, the salesman has done nothing to the size of the value of the article, but he has minimized the size of the price in the prospect's mind. Let us say the price of $12.00 a year was brought down to $1.00 a month, then to 23 cents a week, and then to 3 1/3 cents a day, which is less than the cost of a postage stamp.

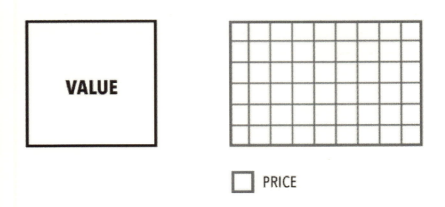

Both methods, of course, can be effectively combined. Some of the classified ads in the newspapers skillfully begin by emphasizing the value of the product and end my minimizing the cost. Here is an advertisement for a used Buick.

BUICK hardtop - 1959. Runs and looks like new. One owner, original white and green paint, whitewalls, R/H, all power, everything. Low mileage. A steal at $950, but must sell. Will finance. NO 7-1234.

Anyone in the market for a used car might well pause at that ad and call the owner. First he tells you what a good car he has for sale, building up all the advantages it offers, and finally he tells you not only that the price is "a steal" but that he will finance it himself so that you can drive it away for only a few dollars a month.

A new magazine opened its advertisement for itself by stating that it brings the reader inside information to be found nowhere else, that it often breaks news before the newspapers, and that it gives the background essential to understanding what is happening in the world. Finally it revealed the price - "less than a penny a day"!

In anything you want to sell, whether it's a small item, a house, or an idea, you can make use of both these methods. Let your prospect know what value you are offering, and show them how little he need give for it.

The transaction must present the prospect's advantage first.

In buying a set of books or a correspondence course, the prospect usually signs an application which states what the prospect must do and what the company will do for him. If this contract is in the form first prepared by the company's lawyer, it will outline, first, all the *obligations* of the purchaser to the company and will state briefly at the end what the purchaser *will get*. The sales department which the prospect signs must enumerate first everything he will get. I should like to explain the importance of this by a story.

In 1946, I negotiated the sale of the controlling stock of the Crosley Corporation to the Aviation Corporation. The top executives and attorneys of both companies spent an entire afternoon in a hotel room, at which I was glad to hear all of the principal points agreed to by all parties. The officers of the Aviation Corporation then left for New York, but the general counsel remained to prepare a contract which I was to get signed by the owner of the Crosley Corporation's stock. The attorney dictated the contract that night. It was typed the next morning, and at 11:00 o'clock I went with him to meet the owner in his attorney's office.

The attorney for the Aviation Corporation had the job, of course, of looking after the interest of his client. That was paramount in his mind. The contract began by stating everything that his company required of the seller. The owner's attorney found fault with these items, and at the close of one hour of such faultfinding, the attorney for "Avco" asked, "Have you changed your mind? Do you people want to sell this or not?"

The owner's attorney said, "Regardless of that question, we certainly are not going to sign any contract with anyone until we are satisfied with it."

The other attorney picked up his papers, telephoned for a Pullman reservation back to New York, went back to the hotel, called the president of the company, explained the situation, and said that in his opinion these people did not want to sell and he was coming home.

The president said, "All right, but let me speak to Clinton." He then told me the attorney was coming back but he said, "Clinton, I want you to stay there and close this deal. Don't come back to New York until it is closed."

Although I had spent two years at law school, I am not an attorney and I do not pretend to know how to draw up a contract as important as this one. However, after studying the contract, I found that it consisted of three parts: (1) several general paragraphs, which included the consideration offered; (2) the requirements on the part of the seller; and (3) the requirements on the part of the purchaser. I called in a stenographer, and merely transposed the positions of number two and number three; that is, immediately following the opening paragraphs. I started by enumerating everything that the seller would get. In other words, I went through the contract and marked "A" opposite every paragraph that was to the advantage of the seller, and all of those paragraphs were placed ahead of the paragraphs that were of advantage to the purchaser.

The next morning I had breakfast with the seller in his home, and told him that I had rewritten the contract to comply with his viewpoint. As he read it, he made remarks similar to, "Now, this is more like it. This is what I want."

I then explained that the board of directors of the purchaser was meeting that afternoon, and that if he signed the contract, I could dictate it to the secretary of the president of the purchasing company by telephone, because she could attach a recorder to her telephone, and the contract could be presented to the board that afternoon. However, if he did not sign it then, the contract could not be presented to the board until thirty-one days had passed. He signed it, I telephoned it, the board agreed, the contract was closed, and my company received a commission of approximately $350,000.

If you do fail, the very fact that you did so may be turned into a steppingstone to greater success.

Convince yourself that every time you lose out it is your fault; that you lost because you failed to present all of the good points, or you did not present them effectively enough, or you failed to ascertain the controlling objection, or you failed to answer that objection satisfactorily.

If you really convince yourself of this, you can then build one of those priceless steppingstones to success. How? By analyzing your failure, not, as in most cases, to find an alibi for your failure, but for the purpose of finding out where you were at fault. You cannot correct your mistakes or overcome your weaknesses until you have found out what they are. If you can then set about correcting them, you can cease stumbling over the difficulties in your way, and begin turning all your obstacles into steppingstones to success.

~ CHAPTER 7 ~

THE LESSON OF THE PILE DRIVER

SOMEONE ONCE SAID that *repetition makes reputation!* And it does. Mr. Dooley, the famous character in the *Chicago Tribune*, once remarked: "I will believe anything if you tell it to me often enough!"

The importance of repetition, of course, is one of the fundamentals of salesmanship. You may have noticed that this book keeps reminding you of those fundamental principles. I learned the importance of doing this from the Bible. There the same principles are repeated again and again. The situation differs; the prophets who deliver the message change; the people to whom the message is addressed vary; but the fundamental message remains unchanged. More than any other book ever published, the Bible has succeeded in getting people to act according to its suggestions. Why? Although its basic truths are few and simple, it has repeated and reiterated them in countless ways from cover to cover.

This principle of repetition, as applied to my business, has increased my earnings and brought me a degree of prosperity I could never have otherwise enjoyed. Practically all my sales in recent years have been made by means of written proposals. When I go back through my files and study those propositions, I find that

I have repeated the same ideas, at least once, in almost every paragraph. After expressing an idea, I would open the next sentence with the phrase "in other words." Then I would present the same idea again, dressed in different words. This does not mean it is wise to repeat words you use; that spells monotony. You can repeat the *ideas* you wish to get across, and if you present them in different words each time you will be able to repeat again and again without any sense of monotony whatever.

Just recently I was asked: 'What makes repetition so powerful a factor in effective suggestion? What purpose does it serve?"

First, the human mind cannot act on what it does not understand. That is why it is so important in whatever you say or write to be crystal-clear. Repetition, especially when it presents a proposition in many ways, serves to make the idea clearer. Suppose you write me a letter. I am not quite sure what you mean, although I believe I know what you are driving at. While I am studying it out, another letter arrives. It repeats the same story in a slightly different way; it gives me a new base-line to think from. I can "triangulate" your meaning and get a surer picture of what you wish to convey. Repetition has done this for me.

Repetition also does something else. It wears down the resisting power of those contrary ideas which entangle your resisting power of those contrary ideas which entangle your idea or suggestion and prevent its ready acceptance by your prospect's mind. Many centuries ago, a man by the name of Job wrote, "The waters wear the stones." That statement is one of the Bible's clearest pictures of the effects of repetition.

Some years ago I read a paragraph about a pile driver which was so true that I clipped it out. Here it is:

No doubt a good many of us have seen a pile-driver machine at its work. Poised in mid-air is the weight or driving part of the machine. Suddenly this weight of several tons is let loose with a deafening noise upon the pile. We would think that the log would be driven down its full length with the terrific impact, but it has hardly moved a fraction of an inch. Again that same terrific impact, and again there is that slight embedment in the ground. And so on this process continues for weeks until the proper foundation is made. It is this cumulative process, this constant hammering, this continuous driving force, that finally erects a foundation upon which to build a permanent structure. It is this same law, this cumulative law, that causes men of obscurity to become famous. It is this steadiness of purpose that lifts men out of the chaos of poverty into the heights of prosperity. It is this sincerity of accomplishment that differentiates between the doer and the wisher.

-Irving Blank

This is why Mr. Dooley will believe anything if he hears it often enough. The pile-driving technique wears out the resisting power of opposing ideas. It helps to make clear what may have been hazy at first. As clarity increases, resistance decreases, and the process of acceptance is rapidly accelerated. The fact that the technique of repetition will convince people of lies as well as truth is of course no excuse for peddling falsehood. As I have tried to point out before, the person who wants to reach the top must make veracity and sincerity his second nature and have nothing to do with untruthfulness. But truth is often crushed to earth, and skillful use of repetition can aid its acceptance.

Earlier in this book I told of attending a school whose president's daily chapel talks made such an impression on my life.

How I Discovered the Secret of Success In The Bible

A large part of my business success I attribute to the influence of those talks by President James Harding, or "Uncle Jimmie" as most of the students affectionately called him. As I look back at my two years in that school, I have tried to analyze what it was that made Uncle Jimmie's words so influential. It was not his oratorical ability, nor his persuasive manner, nor his forceful delivery. Although nearly all the students deeply loved Uncle Jimmie, I do not believe that his warm interest in all of us was the main reason for the way he molded our lives.

In his chapel talks every morning James Harding drove home again and again the fundamental facts of faith in God, the need to serving Him and our fellow men, the possibility of doing big things by His help. I can still hear the way he sued to repeat the Bible: "Whatsoever thy hand finder to do, do it with thy might"; and "I can do all things through Christ which strengtheneth me." I can hear him say, "Start out to be the best man in your line, whatever that may be." I came away from that school with these ideas deeply implanted in my heart and mind. Although it took years for the ideas to germinate and bear fruit, I now realize that what others have called my success is due to the power of those truths from the Bible. And they were driven so deeply into my life by the powerful cumulative effect of the continuous repetition of the same basic ideas.

In my business experience I have found that whenever a proposition is developed by careful repetition of the central thought, it becomes powerfully effective. My prospect may frown in puzzlement the first time he sees an unusual idea in a well-written plan, but by the time he is down to the third paragraph he usually is nodding his head in understanding - often in agreement. By the time he has finished reading, he has a pretty clear conception of the main idea, his natural resistance to a new suggestion is somewhat worn down, and he is more ready to accept my proposition. But every time I fail to repeat the basic thought, I have cause to regret it.

Twenty years after Paul's conversion he made a farewell address to the leaders of the Church of Ephesus, and in it he summarized what he had done to launch the Church throughout the known world. His account is in Acts 20:18-35. He reminded his hearers that he had been with them at all seasons, that he had taught both publicly and from house to house, that he had worked day and night to spread the gospel. And what was his gospel? Two simple ideas which seem to be two sides of the same idea: "repentance toward God, and faith toward our Lord Jesus Christ" (verse 21). That was the thing Paul hammered home to Jews and Gentiles, civilized people and barbarians, year after year. Repeating the same thing over and over - varying the wording, of course, but never changing his gospel - Paul became one of the most successful evangelists of all time.

The pile-driver technique can be a powerful factor in leading the person you want to influence, up the four mental steps from attention to action. Actually getting the decision you want will be discussed in the next chapter.

~ CHAPTER 8 ~

HOW TO GET THE DECISION YOU WANT

ANYONE WHO WANTS to succeed in his work must constantly get other people to make decisions. Every salesman knows that a prospect's attention must be changed to interest in his product, but even though that interest has been built up into a strong desire, there is no sale until the decision is made to buy and the deal is closed. In almost any occupation, however, similar situations continually recur. A person looking for a job must sell his prospective employer on his ability. A man who wants to rent his house must find the kind of tenant he wants and get his decision to rent at the price he thinks appropriate. Artists, writers and musicians are often considered to live on a plane above ordinary mundane affairs, but those who want to make a living must persuade other people to pay them for their creative endeavors. Pastors and evangelists, or course, have emphasized so greatly the importance of getting a decision that "decision" is almost a religious term. Yet everyone must constantly persuade others to come to a decision favorable to his interests. And if you are honest and aboveboard, as you must be for lasting success, the decisions you get other people to make for your own benefit will also benefit them.

      A good batter in a baseball game may win thunderous applause from the grandstands by hitting the ball at a crucial moment, but the score is never marked up in his favor until he gets safely to first base, and second and third and finally home. The fact that he has gone all the way to third base will be of no value whatsoever in winning the game if he stays there. Only when he closes the circuit and makes home base can he help win. And he has to get there safely before the inning ends. Just so, in any transaction all the planning and buildup in the world count for nothing unless you bring the person you are dealing with to the decision you want - at the right time.

One of the most common mistakes made when the time comes to change your prospect's desire into action is the mistake of saying too much. This fact was recognized long ago in the Bible. It is full of counsel concerning the importance of our words and the danger of saying the wrong things, or saying too much. Nearly 3000 years ago a very wise man wrote: "Whoso keepers his mouth and his tongue keepers his soul from troubles" (Proverb 21:23).

I once went to see a prospecting a small town not far from Louisville, Kentucky. He was the only prospect I had in that town. After talking to him for about an hour, he agreed to buy $5,000 worth of insurance from me and said that he had expected to buy from Mid-Western Giant Company. I asked him why.

"Because they have the lowest net cost of any company," he replied.

Although I had already sold him on the idea of buying from my company, I began my rebuttal. "Up in Louisville, Mr. Jones," I said, "there lives a wealthy man who formerly made his home in Milwaukee. He regarded Mid-Western Giant Company very highly, as he should. He refused to buy in any other company. Our agent pointed out to him the cost records of our company and showed him that our cost was lower than Mid-Western. But he refused to believe this. Finally, our agent said, 'Why don't you take $5,000 in each company and check up the cost for several years and find out definitely?' The wealthy man thought this was a good idea. He took $5,000 in each of the companies and has held it for several years. He is now convinced that we have the lowest cost. He has the figures to prove it. I'll gladly give you his name and you can call him on the telephone and verify what I have just told you."

I thought that I had given him a convincing argument to end the idea that Mid-Western had the lowest cost. Here was a well-known man close by whose experience could clinch my case. What could be better proof than that?

My prospect passed the examination and I had the company issue a policy for $5,000 and an additional $5,000 policy, which I felt sure I could sell him. I delivered the ordered policy, and as he was about to write me a check, I began to lay down a barrage of reasons why he should have the whole $10,000. He waited until I paused for breath, then replied: "Yes, I have been thinking over what you said. I guess I should have $10,000 all right [here my heart inserted a couple elated beats], but that Louisville fellow's idea isn't so bad, you know. I've decided to take out $5,000 with you and $5,000 with Mid-Western Giant Company and see how they check up myself! I have already given the Mid-Western Giant Company a prepaid application for a $5,000 policy!"

The idea which I credited for winning the sale had actually cost me the second $5,000. In my effort to prove my point I had introduced a partially contrary idea, and the prospect had acted as much on the contrary idea as he had on the idea which I presented in my own behalf.

That experience taught me not to introduce opposing ideas. It taught me to avoid interjecting any direct suggestion not wholly in line with the action which I wish to bring about. It taught me that selling is as much knowing what *not* to say as it is in knowing what to say.

Let us go back to the simile of the runner at third base. Usually he cannot run home immediately after he reaches third. Certain other events must ordinarily happen before he starts this run. The same is true of the person who has successfully created a desire for what he is trying to sell. Unless certain well-recognized steps are taken after the desire has been created, he very likely will never close the sale, and he is certainly at a great disadvantage if he undertakes to close it before those necessary steps are taken.

The first of these steps, then, is: *Avoid unconsciously picturing ideas contrary to those you want to put across*. Let me illustrate this further. While returning from a western trip one day, I met a chap in the diner on the train and fell into conversation with him. He was a salesman, and was considerably discouraged over the loss of a big order. Somehow or other the conversation turned to selling, and when he found that I was a salesman, too, he broke down and confessed his failure to get this business.

He represented a big Chicago wholesale house. His territory was south of the Ohio River, below Cincinnati. He calls on the small town merchants in that territory perhaps twice a year. Naturally, in his line, he gets some pretty good sized orders. He had this to tell me about the failure from which he was still suffering:

"I was calling on the general store in one of the towns," he began. "There is quite a lot of farming nearby. I checked over the stock and began making out my order. I wasn't loading the owner up, but I was writing down all that I thought he could use. One item after another was put down, priced, and extended. The order was growing rapidly. Finally, when I could think of nothing else, I handed the order to the proprietor to sign. He looked it over, frowned and grumbled a little here and there, but ended up by signing the order. I was elated. It was my biggest order for a month, and I felt pretty cocky. I began to grow talkative. Then, as I picked up my grips to leave, I remarked, "Well, you folks are going to have some nice crops around here this year!"

"Oh, if I only hadn't said it!" groaned my salesman friend. "The storekeeper started to agree with me about the good crops, then stopped in thought. I knew was was going through his mind. 'Are we going to have good crops? Suppose we should have a dry spell like we had three years ago! Where would I sell all this stuff I am buying?' In a flash the damage was done. 'Say, young fellow, let me look at that order I just signed.' I handed it back to him reluctantly, my hear in my mouth. Before he had finished with it, he had reduced the amount of the order by more than half, and instead of my having the best order of the month, I had the smallest order we had taken from him in years. All because I had to shoot off my mouth at the wrong moment and say the wrong thing."

My sympathy went out to this chap, for I have made the same mistake myself. Here another sale was materially reduced because the salesman said the wrong thing at the wrong time and introduced contrary ideas into the prospect's mind.

Many people seem to think they must talk all the time in order to make a sale. That is a mistaken idea. Sometimes the most effective action on the part of a salesman is to be silent while his prospect mentally chews over the proposition he has presented. At such moments the salesman has little chance to know what is going on in the prospect's mind; therefore it is practically impossible to fit his remarks successfully into the prospect's thinking. Often it is better to say nothing in such cases and wait for the prospect to give you your cue. It is a great temptation to a salesman, when the conversation reaches this "vacuum" stage, to say something. But that "something" is a at best only a shot in the dark, and many times it has cost the salesman a sale that he might have won if he had followed the injunction of the Bible, "Whoso keepers his mouth and his tongue keepers his soul from troubles."

While your prospect is on the track, don't derail him. Not long ago we were talking to a man who is very slow to act and who has a reputation of being extremely difficult to sell. We wanted him to invest $100,000 along with other men in exploring for oil. The salesman who brought me to his man was also connected with our Estate Planning business. The man had obviously reached the point where considerable desire had been created. He asked me if I would talk to his tax accountant and auditor. I agreed, but the accountant was out of his office when we telephoned him and we had to wait for him to call back. Before I could start building more desire for oil explorations, our salesman said, "I believe that you will also be interested in our Estate Planning business." Then he started talking to the prospect about it.

We had the prospect on the oil exploration track. He had gone three-fourths of the way and was in line for the station when the salesman tried to derail him. I immediately interrupted and said that this was not the right time to discuss such a large subject, and, without stopping to take a breath, continued building his interest in oil. The accountant returned the call and all three of us went over to his office. Right in the middle of the conversation the salesman said to the accountant, "Because of your vital interest in taxes, I feel certain that you would like to take a few minutes to explain why it will be very helpful to your client who is here with us."

I instantly vetoed that subject on the ground that it would take up too much time, and again, without taking a breath, started talking about closing the oil matter. It is difficult enough to get a check for $100,000 from an individual if you keep him on the track all of the time, but it is practically impossible if you try to derail him and get him started on other tracks.

In my early days, I knew of a salesman whose qualifications for selling exceeded mine in almost every respect, and yet his record was very poor. I couldn't understand it until one day I went on a joint sale with him. Instead of keeping the prospect's mind on one subject, he was continually diverting it. For example, while looking out the prospect's window, he asked him if he knew what kind of car was coming in the gates, and then began talking about the merits of that car, which had no connection whatever with the insurance sale we were trying to make.

One of the great difficulties in bringing a sale to a close is that the prospect or his secretary or the telephone will divert his attention from the subject at hand. That alone makes the situation difficult enough, but when the salesman himself calls attention to other matters, as is so frequently done, and this is added to other diversions, the prospect is completely derailed and never gets into the situation!

I am reminded of the salesman who had secured the prospect's assent and filled out the order blank, which had been signed, and filled out the check for $25,000, and the prospect had the pen in his hand ready to sign. Then he was interrupted by about three telephone calls one after the other. Following the last telephone call, the prospect picked up his pen and began as if to write. Like a pitcher winding up, he made phantom circles over and over again, getting up speed for his Spencerian scrolls. But the pen never touched the paper. The salesman watched in great agony

- the suspense was terrible. Again the pen was poised, and the phantom scrolls began. The salesman could stand it no longer, and in a nervous explosion he exclaimed: "For Pete's sake, write!"

Probably the most important thing to remember just before closing is that the mind of the prospect swings like a pendulum from negative to positive and back again to negative before the sale is closed. A friend of mine, Will Beers, who was probably the greatest salesman ever known in the city of Rochester, New York, did quite a bit of practical research on selling. One of his discoveries was that before making a sale which involves a large amount of money or a big idea, the pendulum swings in a definite pattern. At first the prospect's reaction is negative. He has no intention of buying the product or the idea, but after the salesman has reached the point where considerable desire has been attained, the mind of the prospect is in a positive position. But just before the time for the decision, doubts arise. The pendulum swings back to the negative. The prospect begins to ask himself questions such as this: "What the salesman says sounds good, but how certain can I be that he is telling the entire story?" Or this: "After I buy this I will not be dealing with the salesman, I will be dealing with the company. How strong is this company financially? What is its reputation for fair dealing? Will it take advantage of technicalities?"

The salesman should realize that under normal circumstances these doubts will arise when the prospect is almost ready to close. Therefore, in planning a sales presentation he should provide the right answers for this time. This is a good place to bring in a brief summary of the sales talk, to offer proof regarding the soundness, safety and certainty of the plan, and to stress the fact that there is no chance for the prospect to lose. If sufficient confidence is built at this time, the doubts subside, the pendulum swings back to the positive, and the prospect is ready to close. Very few large sales are consummated before the pendulum has swung from negative to positive, then just before the close, back to the negative, and then after being reassured, back to the positive.

Here is a method by which a sole salesman I know gets action. After he has tried various styles and sizes on the customer, he picks up the shoes which he thinks the customer prefers, mentions something favorable about them, and asks, "Would you care to wear these home, or shall we send them?" That is called "Getting the decision on a minor point," because whichever answer the prospect gives, the sale has been made.

Back in the days when the doctors gave such evil-tasting medicines, my wife and I used that method on our son. We would say to him, "The doctor left this medicine and you can either take it or you can take castor oil." Naturally, he always took the medicine the doctor left. He chose what was to him the lesser of two evils! The "either-or" principle gets the decision.

The actual technique of closing is not as important as the material you have just read. In most cases there is no difficulty whatever in closing if two things have happened first: (1) a strong desire has been built; (2) the obstacles have been removed.

Obviously, it is desirable for the salesman to be in command at all times. Let me show you through an interesting and true story how dangerous it is for the salesman to let the prospect take command.

At the time that I moved to New York City, Hal Reed represented The Banker's Trust Company of 14 Wall Street. Mr. Reed's job was the solicitation of business for his trust division. At that time, the Chairman of the Board of the Banker's Trust was

Seward Prosser, who had formerly been a general agent for the Equitable Life Assurance Society. Mr. Prosser had a splendid sales personality and also had made quite a record in the sale of life insurance before J. P. Morgan asked him to head The Banker's Trust Company. Hal Reed told me that the method he had used most successfully in getting very wealthy people to name The Banker's Trust Company as executor and trustee was that of inviting the prospect to have luncheon at The Banker's Trust Company with Mr. Prosser and himself. He explained, "Mr. Prosser is just about then times as good as I am in selling these ideas."

At that time The Banker's Trust Company was engaged in materially enlarging its building at 14 Wall Street. Mr. Reed succeeded in getting Thomas J. Watson, of the International Business Machines Corporation, to have luncheon with Mr. Prosser and himself for the purpose of learning how The Banker's Trust Company could best serve Mr. Watson.

Tom Watson was for many years called the greatest salesman in the world, and the growth of his company indicates that this statement cannot be far wrong. Hal told me that while The Banker's Trust Company building was being extensively enlarged, it could be greatly improved by installing IBM clocks in all the offices.

Hal said that from then on the conversation revolved around the great advantages of having these clocks and that at the end of the meeting, Mr. Prosser had agreed that the clocks should be installed. But not one word had been said about the advantages of the trust services of The Banker's Trust Company.

I rented one of these offices for my business, and every time I looked up at the IBM clocks, I was reminded of Mr.

Prosser's efforts to sell Mr. Watson, which resulted in Watson selling Prosser. Two men each planned to influence the other to do the thing he wanted him to do, and the better man won.

In most cases, the salesman should not wait for the prospect to take the initiative, but should direct the prospect's action. There are exceptions. In some of the largest cases I have ever sold I've reached the closing point and then sat perfectly still, waiting for the prospect to voice his decision.

~ CHAPTER 9 ~

BECOME THE GREATEST IN YOUR FIELD

A. T. STEWART became the first great merchant prince of America because he followed the advice of Jesus as to how to be greatest in our field. Shortly afterward Marshall Field built the largest department store in the world on the same principle.

Unfortunately many people seem able to make only limited progress toward success. Even though the have learned all the principles explained up to this point, they are able to sell small ideas only. The question then arises, "How does one learn to become the greatest in his field?" The answer is extremely simple and it was given by Jesus.

James and John once asked Jesus for the two highest places in the Kingdom. When the other ten Apostles were displeased at the request, Jesus said, "Whosoever will be great among you, shall be your master: And whosoever of you will be the chiefest, shall be servant of all" (Mark 10:43-44). *He who would be greatest of all must be servant of all.*

Some people say, "The Bible is all right except that it's out of date. We have progressed too much to follow those old-fashioned ideas now." But the fact is that the Bible was more out of date at the time it was written thousands of years ago than it is today. Jesus' statement about becoming greatest must have seemed much more foolish to the leaders of His day than to our own present-day leaders. The businessmen in the time of Jesus had as their motto *Caveat emptor* - "Let the Buyer Beware." They were not ashamed of it. They thought that the way to be great in business was to be tricky, to be dishonest, to make all that you could out of one customer with no regard to truthfulness. They said of the buyer, "If he's taken in, it's his fault. You are not supposed to protect the buyer. If you tell the buyer that a cotton cloth is linen and he believes you, he is just a sucker."

Caveat emptor was also the established business motto for hundreds of years after the death of Jesus, although Jesus taught differently. He said, "He that would be greatest among you, let him become the servant of all." Do you think that any of the business leaders of the day believed that? No! Not then and not for at least 1800 years. Businessmen said that His teaching might be all right for religion but business was business and therefore Jesus' principle could not be used in business.

After my father's death, my mother worked in a department store named "The Golden Rule." Its name today is "Stewart's." My mother was told to lie about the merchandise she sold. She was instructed to say, "This is 100 per cent linen," when it was not. Nearly all stores practiced that principle at that time. Her employer said she was employed to make all the money she could for the store - that and nothing more. That was the policy, the same "buyer beware" policy that was in effect in the time of Jesus. Today, in that store, anyone who lied about its merchandise would be fired. What brought about the change?

A young merchant in New York City be the name of A. T. Stewart somehow or other got the idea that the way to get ahead was not *Caveat emptor*, but service. He decided to start a store where the entire policy would be that of serving the customers. He questioned his customers continually as to the type of merchandise they liked, the type of service they wanted, etc. He was meticulously honest; his principles were all based upon *service* and he built the first great department store in America.

When Mr. Stewart died, the store was purchased by John Wanamaker of Philadelphia. For years and years, it still managed to attract them, largely because of the reputation that had been built up by Mr. Stewart who said, "I'm going to build a store on a new motto: 'He that would have the greatest store, let him be the greatest servant to his customers.'" Mr. Stewart also said, "No abilities, however splendid, can command success without intense labor and persevering application." This paraphrased the Bible verse, "Whatsoever they hand finder to do, do it with thy might." Mr. Stewart had read his Bible.

Shortly after A. T. Stewart picked that motto, a young boy came over from Scotland to Chicago and started to work at $3.00 a week. He also believed in that motto. Later on, he applied the same principle to his business, using different words. His motto was, "The customer is always right." All clerks were instructed that whenever a customer brought back merchandise, they were to refund the money without objection. And, as you probably know, very often customers returned merchandise by mistake which they had purchased in other stores. When they brought it back to Marshall Field's, the clerks took it back and refunded their money. They followed the principle that if you want to have the greatest store, you must offer the greatest service, and so Marshall Field, the little Scotch immigrant boy who started to work in this country at $3.00 a week, built the greatest department store in the world. He was the second leader in the department store field to try out the principle that Jesus gave over 1900 years ago.

A business can never become successful merely by making one sale to each customer. Success depends upon repeat sales. Repeat sales depend upon the customer being satisfied, and satisfaction results from service. The *permanent* success of any business, therefore, results from what Jesus taught as essential: serving.

Emerson said that every service brings its own reward. Unfortunately, many people still believe that the reward from service comes only in the after-life. A. T. Stewart and Marshall Field demonstrated that there are rewards here and now.

Many years ago Mr. Post used the idea of service to build up a business specializing in such foods as Postum and Post's Bran Flakes. As this business became successful, Mr. Post decided to use some of the profits to help others. He bought thousands of acres of land in Texas and then sold the land on the installment basis to poor individuals who wanted to farm. He purchased one block of 5,000 acres and then sold 100 acres each to 50 individuals at the original cost to him, permitting them to pay for it over a period of years. It did not work out as he planned. He was not able to sell some of the land and a good number of purchasers changed their minds and the property reverted to him. In addition to the time and energy spent on the project, it also cost him a small fortune. His friends kidded him about the matter, saying "That's what always happens to one who tries to be a 'do-gooder.' " But this act of service on his part brought in a substantial reward. His widow is today receiving very large royalties from the oil that was later discovered on this land.

The service principle applies in every position in life, high or low. I had a partner for some years who was very difficult to please. He seldom kept a secretary longer than one year. Nevertheless, over a period of twenty years we did have in the organization two secretaries who served him so well that he said they were the best he had ever had. The parents of one secretary came to this country from Russia and served for many years as missionaries among the Russian people who worked in the Chicago stockyards. When her mother and father called upon these immigrants who lived in the slum district, this girl washed the dishes and helped clean up the house; she was taught from infancy that happiness comes though serving others. When she became secretary to an important man, she looked upon the position as an opportunity to serve. The other secretary was the daughter of a very poor Baptist minister. She was brought up in a similar environment and was imbued with the same principles.

One of our investment counsel clients, a man who paid me $75,000 per year for advice, was worth in excess of $150,000,000. When I first met him he had an income of approximately $2,000,000 per year, and I was amazed to find that he was giving away 100 per cent of his income. After working with him closely for about a year, he told me at lunch one day how he happened to be giving all of his income away.

He had inherited a fortune made in this country, but when he was a young boy he was sent to England to be educated. This resulted in his having close friends among the most important people in England, including the royal family. Later on, when he came into his inheritance, this tremendous fortune gave him an outstanding position in the United States. With an unusually attractive personality and polished continental manners, he was recognized by many as having the top-level social position both in the United States and in England, but he said to me:

"Clinton, I was unhappy - completely miserable - all of the time. After marrying, I was still unhappy. My wife and I thought that if we built exactly the kind of home he wanted we would be content. So we purchased a thousand acres on Long Island and spent $6,000,000 building our dream palace. But we were still unhappy. At last I thought that a divorce would correct the situation; but it didn't. Later I married again and found things even worse than during my first marriage, and so a second divorce was secured. Shortly after that, I slowly realized that I was beginning to drink in the morning, and when you start drinking in the morning, that's bad! A friend of mine suggested that I see a psychiatrist named Dr. Gregory Zilboorg. In telling the doctor about my case, I mentioned that the happiest years I could remember were during the First World War. My friends urged me to go to officers' training school, but I preferred entering as a private. I could not understand why I should have been happier as a private in the army than I had been either before or after the war, while surrounded by my friends.

"Dr. Zilboorg said that it was perfectly understandable to him: "The only way anyone can find happiness is by serving others. All of your life, except during the time you spent in the army, you were surrounded by people who were anxious to serve you. The situation was reversed, however, when you entered the army as a private. There you had to serve others. I suggest that you select a charity in which you can render personal service and you will find that the degree of your happiness will depend upon the extent to which you are serving others.'

"I discussed the subject with the welfare board of the City of New York and decided to work with and help Negro boys in Harlem. In addition to this, I decided to give my income quietly and anonymously in the manner which I thought was best calculated to help others." And then my friend said: "Clinton, I have been one of the happiest men in the world ever since I started following Dr. Zilboorg's advice."

Of course, this advice did not originate with Dr. Zilboorg. It came from the lips of the Great Physician Himself almost 2,000 years ago!

"Do you want to be the greatest lawyer in this state?" I asked a young law student. "You can be. Just prepare yourself to render greater service to your clients than any other lawyer in this state. If you get to where you are rendering greater service to your clients than any other lawyer, you will become the greatest lawyer in this state."

Do you want to be the greatest physician, or the greatest surgeon? It is very simple. A friend on mine was operated on in the Presbyterian Hospital about a month ago and the surgeon's bill was $6,000. Why was he able to charge and collect $6,000 for one operation? Because his patients believe that he can render a service that no one else can.

If you want to become the greatest in your field, no matter what it may be, equip yourself to render greater service than anyone else. I know you will succeed, because Jesus promised it.

And if you follow the principles He emphasized, you will become a "one-eyed man." What I mean by that I must explain in the next chapter, for it is so important that I have a lot to say about it.

~ CHAPTER 10 ~

BE A ONE-EYED MAN

YOU HAVE PROBABLY often heard the proverb, "Don't put all your eggs in one basket." There is some wisdom in that. But I like better what Andrew Carnegie once said: "Put all thine eggs in one basket and - *watch that basket*." (This saying is also attributed to Mark Twain.) One thing well done is worth a million things poorly done. It is still true that the jack of all trades is usually master of none.

Thirty years ago I got into the business of producing educational motion pictures. The venture was supposed to cost a few thousand dollars, but when the bills were all in, the cost was seven times the estimate. My part of that obligation had to be met, yet only a fraction of the cash was on hand with which to do it. I had two options: I could go out and dig up the money, or I could default on the obligation and take the consequences. I chose the first way.

There was one insurance case on which I had been working for months. It was probably the "meanest" case I ever had. The prospect was a newly rich Prussian, domineering and overbearing. He abused me, browbeat me and treated me shamefully. But I had submitted the plan which covered his needs perfectly. He needed to place that plan in operation. There wasn't any question in my mind about it.

When this large financial demand crashed suddenly down on me, I said to myself, "There is only one place I can get that much money quickly; that is the Von Hoss case. It has been hanging fire for months. Now, I'll have to close it." I put on my hat, got my brief case, and told my wife goodbye. "I'm going out to see Mr. Von Hoss," I told her, "and I'm going to have a showdown. Either I make it or break it today." I completed the transaction that day and got the check for it. I had plenty of money to pay off my obligation and some to put in the bank. The crises was licked.

It happened that this case was the only big one I had on the fire at that time. If I had had a dozen cases, I would not have gone to see Mr. Von Hoss that day. And probably I would have let the case drag along until I lost it. From that experience, I learned two things: First, keep out of the other fellow's business and stay in your own business where you know your way around. Second, devote your entire energy to one thing at a time.

One evening while reading the Book of books I ran across tow verses that set me to thinking. One was from Philippians 3:13: "This one thing I do, forgetting those things which are behind, and reaching forth unto those things which are before, I press toward the mark." The second verse was: "The light of the body is the eye: if therefore thine eye be single, they whole body shall be full of light" (Matthew 6:23).

If thine eye be single… I thought of a young man hunting squirrels with a .22 rile. Just as he gets a bead on a squirrel he hears some girls laughing. He looks around and see that they are swimming in a pond nearby. He tries to keep one eye on the squirrel and one eye on the girls. That squirrel doesn't need any life insurance! There is no danger of his being hit by that .22. The way to get the squirrel is to close one eye and keep the other eye on the squirrel at the end of the line of vision from the rifle sights. I resolved to become a one-eyed man.

I thought of the men who had accomplished the most in history. Abraham, Moses, David, Elijah, Paul - all were men with an eye single to the task, their whole bodies and personalities filled with light. Abraham Lincoln was a one-eyed man, or he would never have said, "I'll fight it out on this line if it takes all summer."

A situation arose which gave me the opportunity to carry out my resolve to be a one-eyed man. The life insurance company I represented as general agent wanted me to secure a large number of mediocre agents. I wanted a few outstanding large-production salesmen. The superintendent of agencies issued an ultimatum giving me three months to secure four agents of mediocre type. I did not believe in this method, so I resigned, and immediately started out for myself, working on a brokerage basis which permitted me to select the policy and company best suited to my clients' needs.

But one of the agents to whom I had been paying a drawing account insisted on going along. "I am sticking with you," he informed me. So I had *his* grocery bill, as well as my own, and also my office expenses and my stenographer's salary to worry about. I added up to more than $1,000 a month - and I had less than $300.00 cash in the bank. Like every general agent, my capital was tied up in the business and was represented by commissions to be paid in the future - over a nine-year period!

I remembered what Christ had said: "If thine eye be single, they whole body shall be full of light." So I decided to be a "one-eyed man."

There was one wealthy man on my list whose age was soon to change. That meant, of course, that his premium rate would advance. Such dates, in the insurance business, are used by every agent to force a quick close on pending business. But that gave me no exclusive advantage. Almost every insurance agent in town knew about this man's birthday, and all but a couple of cripples were trying to sell him insurance before that day swung around.

I made up my mind that, for this month, I had only one prospect - this man. I resolved that "this one thing" I would do.

It was fortunate that I made that decision. Why? Because the man was the most difficult individual in town to see. He kept no regular hours. Although he spent from thirty minutes to an hour each day in his office, no one ever knew when that would be. I did not let this irritate me. Since he had become my one and only prospect for that month, I arrived at his office early every morning with plenty of reading matter. Several days I stayed all day. It took several interviews to close the sale, and I managed to secure those interviews because each time I was on hand the entire day. The other salesman could not wait because they had fifty or more prospects to see that month.

As we were riding in my new client's car on the way to the medical examiner's, he said to me, "You are the most persistent man I have ever seen. Quite a few insurance agents know that my rate increases this month. They have written letters and left their telephone numbers, but I haven't seen them. You did not get this business because your company is any better than the others. You got it because you got your message before me often enough."

My commissions on his business were over $2,000. The problems of my representative's salary, my own living expenses, my office rent and my stenographer's salary were all solved for a couple of months, at least. By being a determined "one-eyed man," I had made more money for myself than if I had been flitting here and there, working half-heartedly on fifty different cases.

Many years' experience since that incident have convinced me that being a one-eyed man helps a great deal. I have gone for months at a time with only one prospect on my list. I have spent weeks and months working out a plan with that one prospect. But the case was large - and when it was closed, I was handsomely paid for the weeks and months I had spend on it. My associate and I sold one man $5,000,000 of ordinary life and singe-premium insurance. His age was 59. We worked continuously for six months before closing this case, but the commissions were more than the average agent earned in ten years.

A man selling big cases (and I think this is true as well of any other man in business) needs two capacities: the capacity to separate the good from the bad, the big from the little, and the capacity to concentrate on the big and the good until he sells them or definitely loses them.

Suppose that you decided to follow this procedure. You would need some capital, and some confidence in yourself, in God, and in the future. If you said to me: "I haven't the capital now," I would say, "Start being a one-eyed man anyhow. Pick out your best case, however poor it looks, and concentrate on it. You will be surprised how much headway you will make and how quickly you will close it. If you should happen to lose it, don't stop to weep over that. Take the best remaining case. This plan never fails to produce good results for me. You may not guess the best case the first time, or you may fail to sell the first case you select as being best. But if you stick to the principle of being a one-eyed man, you will win. Nothing can stop you!"

A large New Jersey life insurance company asked me to address a convention of their Kentucky representatives on the subject of "The One-Eyed Man." One of the men in the audience, Joe Weill, although only a part-time representative, wrote about the same amount of life insurance per year that I did when I represented that company in Kentucky. His real job was that of cashier of a bank in Owensboro, Kentucky. But, in addition to this, he wrote a reasonable amount of life insurance, managed the Opera House, the local baseball team, and also managed to take care of a few other responsibilities. In my address, I referred to the necessity of devoting all of one's time, energy and thought to *one* responsibility, and thereby doing that better than anyone else in the world, using as illustrations such men as Henry Ford, E. H. Harriman and Thomas A. Edison.

At the close of the address, Joe came up to see me and said, "Clint, you have converted me. From now on I intend to be a one-eyed man." He resigned from the bank and devoted all of his time, thought and energy to his life insurance company. The result was that he wrote at least one life insurance application each week consecutively for one thousand weeks. Although Owensboro had a population of only 23,000, he wrote over $10,000,000 of life insurance after he became a "one-eyed man."

There was another crisis in my affairs shortly after I moved to New York. It came about because I was lured away from my resolve to concentrate on one thing only at a time. I had previously gone into another business, put up a lot of money, obligated myself for still more, and, to make the sad story short, I had lost it all. I realized that I must advertise if I was to make any headway in New

York. I had a book which I wished to publish at my own expense to be used to help secure prospects. I had to engage some "bird dogs" to point up prospects for me. I had to have an office, and an office meant employees and expenses - large expenses, such as I had not had before. And I had less than $500.00 in the bank.

I returned to my resolution to be a one-eyed man. The resolution was much more determined now, enforced by my recent losses. I went over my list of prospects. In my former city was a wealthy client whose needs for insurance had never been fully met. He had the money to pay for more coverage, too, which was highly important to me.

One of Mr. Pullman's sleepers landed me in the city the next morning, and, before noon, I was laying my plan before my prospect. The sale was not difficult. I had his confidence from previous dealings. The need for additional insurance was quite apparent. He signed the application for $300,000 of insurance. My potential commissions were $10,000. I took the doctors to his office, saw the examination completed, patted myself on the back and said: "Well, old man, there's $10,000 which ought to last us for a few months." With that, I went to Atlantic City with my wife for a week's rest.

But my holiday was short-lived. One of the companies called for an additional specimen of urine and I received a phone call from the medical director saying that in the course of the urinalysis they had found a trace of sugar. Now, "sugar" in the medical parlance usually means diabetes, and diabetes, to the insurance agent, means no policies issued and no commissions paid.

I took the next train to that city. Meanwhile, some further specimens had been submitted which showed no sugar. Here was an intermittent sugar condition that life insurance companies at the time did not want to take a chance on. One company, however, had made exhaustive studies of diabetes and I knew that if I could get that company to accept the risk, the other companies would quite likely fall in line. I went to the medical director of this company. "There is only one chance," he said, and then he explained a long and tedious examination which would give a sugar determination that left no doubt. "But," warned the medical director, "the applicant has to stay in our examiner's office for four hours while the test is going on, and there isn't one man in a thousand show will do it."

"This man will do it," I replied, "because I have only one thing to do and that is to get him there and get the matter completed."

The medical director's pessimism did not dismay me. I went to my client's office, knowing that I had ahead of me a much bigger selling job than when I was merely persuading him to buy the insurance. Now I had to persuade him - the president of three successful companies - to go to the medical examiner's office and sit for more than four hours while a tedious test was being made requiring several extractions of blood.

He was in his office. I stated the facts, then said: "Now, you don't have to go though with this if you prefer not to, but what do you say, *let's show these fellows they're wrong!*"

That was the right appeal. The challenge to show the doctors that they were mistaken about this man's condition aroused in him the fighting instinct that exists in practically every man. He put on his hat and went to the medical referee's office with me. There he sat for more than four hours, talking to me, reading, submitting to the tests. Of course, I did not leave him. I stayed with him every moment.

Later, when the tests were reported upon, the medical director said, "Well, we will accept your risk. We are having the policies issued." I immediately telephoned the news to the other companies and asked them to verify it by telephoning this medical director. Instead of selling $300,000 - the amount originally applied for - I sold him $700,000, the commissions amounting to almost $25,000 instead of $10,000. The average policy sold in 1927 by the average agent with a horde of prospects amounted to $2,500. In other words, I made as much money on this case as I would have made on 280 average cases, and nobody claims to be able to sell 280 contracts in one month. This sale put an end to may financial crises for a long time.

It also did something else: It showed me more clearly than ever that to succeed it is absolutely necessary to be a one-eyed man. And anyone with normal capacities can succeed in any line of work if he will follow the course of the Apostle Paul, saying, "This one thing I do!"

~ CHAPTER 11 ~

THE POWER OF SUGGESTION

SEVERAL MEN ARE standing at a soda fountain. One says, "I'm thirsty. I want something to drink."

Another says, "All right, we'll keep you company. What shall we have?"

The first one says, "I don't care, just so it is wet."

But as they are discussing the subject of quenching their thirst, all of them are looking at a sign which reads, "Drink Coca-Cola." Someone says, "Let's have a Coke."

So the decision is made, not by reason, nor by argument, nor by coercion. The decision is made purely on the basis of *suggestion*.

How many millions of times that scene has been enacted at a soda fountain is anyone's conjecture. The important thing is, long ago someone came up with that advertisement consisting of three words. No reason is given for the suggestion. The advertisement does not say it is good. It does not say that Coca-Cola is healthful. It does not say it is economical. It just says, "Drink Coca-Cola!"

Later the copy writers even economized on words and shortened the suggestion too, "Have a Coke!" And countless millions of people have yielded to the power of that suggestion and just stepped up to a side fountain and said without knowing why they said it, "Give me a Coke."

Suggestion is probably one of the most powerful forces in the world. Generally, it falls under two headings: suggestions we make to others, and suggestions that we make to ourselves. The latter is called "autosuggestion."

Before we are able to practice the power of suggestion on others, we must learn how he used this power of suggestion on himself in order to accomplish a task which was extremely difficult for him to get started on. My friend had another job, and, at the time of the incident of which he told me, he was supplementing his regular income by selling Analytical Bibles. As long as he concentrated on selling Bibles, he made good. He was an able salesman and could speak convincingly of his product, for he knew it. But his other duties would often interfere, and sometimes he would be out of the selling business for several days at a time.

On one occasion he was interrupted to such an extent that he did not get out to sell Bibles for two or three weeks. In the meantime, he had lost his stride, the sales drive within him had weakened, and he found himself actually dreading to go out and trying to sell a Bible. However, Old Lady Necessity was catching up with him, and he knew that something had to be done.

My friend had found that he was most successful when he set a goal of Bible sales by the dozen. He never considered one sale as accomplishing his objective; he had to sell a dozen in a particular group before he would rest. So it wasn't merely a matter of his stepping out and finding a prospect to buy a Bible that he was facing at this time. He knew when he started that he would have to sell a dozen, and he had to drive himself to launch out toward that objective.

Here is what my friend did to get himself started. He sat down and took several small index cards and with his pen wrote on those cards, "Sell Analytical Bibles." That is all he wrote, just those three words. He place one card in the mirror above his dresser so he would see it every time he stepped up to comb his hair. He placed one over the washbasin in the bathroom so he would have to see it every time he went in to wash his face. He put one of them in his pocketbook so every time he pulled out his pocketbook there stared at him his own suggestion: "Sell Analytical Bibles!" He distributed these cards all around the room and on his person, and then he set in to wait to see what would happen. That day passed, and he hadn't sold a Bible. The next day came, and he was still busy, too busy to get out and sell Bibles. But the power of suggestion was continually pounding on his consciousness: "Sell Analytical Bibles!"

On the third day after he wrote these suggestions, he got out of bed, dressed, and went out to find his first prospect. He found the prospect, sold a Bible, and he was in business again. Within two days, he had reached his goal, sold his dozen Bibles and had kept up his other work besides. Now, although I don't recommend dividing your interest as my friend did, I believe this shows how you can use the power of autosuggestion to accomplish what you want done.

The ninth chapter of Matthew gives us a great example of how a sorely afflicted woman was healed of a hemorrhage from which she was dying. She had had this hemorrhage for twelve years. She had exhausted all the resources of her doctors, but had never improved. As a matter of fact, the Bible says that she was getting worse all the time.

The woman heard about Jesus, that He was healing people. Undoubtedly she felt unworthy to go to Him and present her case directly. She may also have felt unable to do so, but she found a point of contact. Matthew says, "*For she said within herself,* If I may but touch his garment, I shall be whole." Notice that this woman sold herself on the idea that she would be well the moment she touched Jesus' robe. She did not allow for progressive improvement, but expected instantaneous healing, and that is exactly what she got.

You will notice, also, that she said this "within herself." That is, she used the most powerful form of autosuggestion. What we say audibly has its effect, and sometimes it may be necessary for us to make our suggestions audibly in order to condition our subconscious mind to receive them. This is particularly true when our thinking has been negative and full of fear in the past. But when we get to the place that we can converse with ourselves by simply speaking within our own hearts, we are then practicing the most powerful and the most irresistible form of autosuggestion.

There were difficulties that had to be faced by this afflicted woman, but what she had told her heart conditioned her to face and *overcome* those difficulties. She had to get through the crowd to find Jesus. She actually must have had to crawl part of the way, for when she got to Him, she did not touch His sleeve, or His collar, or His hand. She touched the hem of His robe; she must have been down on her hands and knees.

What could have kept a poor, sick woman like this going forward in the face of such almost insurmountable obstacles? There is only one thing: she had convinced herself that she could do it. She believed that in her touch of the robe of Jesus she would find instant healing. She pressed through the throng, reached Him, brushed her fingers lightly against the hem of His garment, and instantly the hemorrhage was stopped.

Effective salesmanship springs from a fountain of positive suggestions. And not the least important are these suggestions that we make to ourselves. A Jewish rabbi who was also a life insurance salesman made the statement that while on the way to an important sales interview he always repeated the Twenty-third Psalm. The result was that when he faced the prospect he had a quiet, calm feeling of confidence which helped him immeasurably in the interview.

Some years ago I asked a professor who has written textbooks on suggestion, "What is the world's masterpiece of autosuggestion?"

After thinking about my question for a while he agreed that there was no question about the answer. "The Twenty-third Psalm," he said, "is undoubtedly the world's masterpiece."

This Psalm has comforted many in time of sickness. It is used at funerals more than any other Scripture. It has been memorized by millions of people; probably no other chapter in the Bible is so well known. Alcoholics have been cured after repeating it daily for a specified period of time.

Let us look at the Twenty-third Psalm and see what it tells us. Please pay special attention to the words that are italicized.

"The Lord is *my* shepherd."

Who is my shepherd? God, the all-powerful Creator of the entire universe. This means that He leads me, and if I follow Him, He will take care of me just as a good shepherd provides for all the needs of his sheep. It follows, therefore, that, "*I* shall not want."

There was scarcity of food in those days, and starvation was not unknown. Think of these words: "He maketh *me* to lie down in green pastures." The food, the best possible food for the sheep, is all around them. After they have eaten their fill, they actually lie down and wallow in it. Are the sheep worried? Never, if they have a good shepherd. Today, anyone who can say "The Lord is *my* shepherd" should not have to rely on sleeping pills to relax.

David speaks of green pastures. How restful and soothing is green. I know of a corporation where the directors fought one another at every board meeting, and yet when outside of the board meeting they seemed to get along with each other wonderfully. Finally an expert in psychology was employed to investigate and find out why they fought at the meetings. The psychologist called their attention to the fact that the carpet, the draperies, and all the furnishings in the board room were red. He suggested that they change to a color of green. He said that red is an inciting color, whereas green is a relaxing color. The change was made and the fighting at board meetings ceased.

"He leaders *me* beside the still waters." In mountainous country many of the mountain streams cut down deep so that sheep cannot reach the water, but if they have a good shepherd, all is well. The shepherd knows the watering places and arranges so that they reach a place of still water in the right time.

"He restoreth *my* soul." Sheep, like people, sometimes refuse to follow the feet of the shepherd. We think that we know better than the shepherd. So the sheep sometimes find the wrong path, and find themselves in a ravine or pit out of which they cannot get unaided. The shepherd always seeks out such strays and restores them.

"Yea, though *I* walk through the valley of the shadow of death, *I* will fear no evil, for thou art with *me*." Even in the darkest times, the most fearful experiences, and the roughest places of life, we can live without fear if we know that the God of the universe is our Shepherd.

"Thy rod and thy staff they comfort *me*." The shepherd's staff served not only as an instrument by which he could extricate the sheep from dangerous places, but as a rod of correction. The Lord's protection may sometimes seem like a rod upon our backs, but He is too good to do a wrong, too wise to make a mistake.

"Thou prepares a table before *me* in the presence of *mine* enemies." The sheep in David's day had plenty of enemies. There were snakes, bears, mountain lions, poisonous weeds, unscrupulous robbers and bandits. All of these threatened the lives of the sheep, but with a good shepherd they feared no evil. Although they had to live their lives, eat their food, and get their rest in the very presence of their enemies, they could do so with calmness and confidence. Their shepherd saw to their safety.

"Thou anointest *my* head with oil; *my* cup runneth over." There is assurance for the sheep with a good shepherd. His wounds are healed. His strength is restored. He is surrounded with abundance.

"Surely goodness and mercy shall follow *me* all the days of *my* life: and *I* will dwell in the house of the Lord *forever*." We can be confident that the goodness of God will never desert us. A

Scottish preacher told his flock, "The Lord is my shepherd, aye, and more than that, he has twa fine collie dogs, Goodness and Mercy. With him before and them behind, even poor sinners like you and me can hope to win home at last." The Lord is with us all the days of this life, and will be forevermore.

Surely you will agree this is the world's masterpiece of autosuggestion. My! what tremendous mental and spiritual power is packed into the Twenty-third Psalm!

In *The Sword Arm of Business* by Theodore MacManus is this statement about suggestion (although I have taken the liberty to change the word "advertising" to "persuasion"):

When we seek the one great fundamental which underlies the principle and practice of persuasion, we need go no further than the simple, psychological fact that people are susceptible to suggestion. We live, move, and have our being in a swirl of suggestion from morning till night, and from the age of reason to the edge of the grave. Seldom are those suggestions systematic or scientific. They are floating, vagrant, intermittent - and still they rule the lives of millions. Now suppose them to be systematic, instead of irregular; scientific, instead of incidental. Suppose their application to be subtle, continuous, persistent. Can any sane man question the result?

I do not need to point out to you that this thinker knows the Bible. You undoubtedly have already discovered this from his use of Paul's phrase, "We live, and move, and have our being."

In former times it was believed that the human mind was influenced mainly by logic, argument, and reason. But recently it has been observed that men who used illogical reasoning, or no reasoning at all, were often able to get more action from people than those who depended upon reason. Within the past sixty years this extra-logical force has been identified as *suggestion*. Suggestion differs from argument in two ways: 1) argument must be expressed in language, whereas suggestion may be expressed in either words or in action, and oftentimes it is most effective when no words are used; 2) argument must be supported by proof or reasons, whereas suggestion, to be effective, need offer no reason whatsoever.

Years ago, the United States Tire Company used for its principal advertisement a short, positive sentence which contained a powerful suggestion: "United States Tires are good tires!" No reason was given *why* they where good tires. No proof was produced. That one simple, direct, positive suggestion was repeated over and over.

In one of my classes on salesmanship, I had for a student a salesman from this tire company. I asked this student one day whether they had any evidence of the effectiveness of this one sentence. He replied, "Yes indeed we have! I quite often repeat it myself to dealers and others to whom I am selling. I will say, 'Well, you know United States Tires are good tires,' and their reply will invariably be in substance, 'Oh, yes, we know they are good tires!' "

A mother left home for an afternoon of shopping downtown. A few minutes before she left, the grocer had delivered a can of unground coffee. She warned the children as she left, "Don't you children open that coffee and put any of those coffee beans up your nose." Although the children had never before thought of putting coffee beans up their nostrils, they were doing it five minutes after mother left. Why? The idea had been implanted, and it was expanding like a coiled spring in their minds, compelling them to act according to its power, and contrary to their mother's command. In other words, her suggestion was more powerful than her *authority*.

In Tennessee's history there was a politician who invariably removed his coat before making his speeches. He always saw to it on such occasions that one suspender button was missing. This man was elected to the office of governor of his state, and his name has come down in Tennessee's history as the "one-gallus" Governor. And in Georgia, Governor Eugene Talmadge won a warm place in the hearts of his people by wearing red suspenders! This use of suggestion was so powerful that even after he had been dead for a number of years all the members of the state legislature wore red suspenders at one session. Suggestion may sometimes be bizarre, but do not discount its effectiveness if you wish to achieve success.

Shortly after I came to New York, I was able to write a $500,000 policy on the life on one of the leading real estate men of the United States. This man's company was manager for many of the large buildings in New York City. Although the policy was on his life, it was to be paid for by the XYZ company. At the time my client was examined, he said, "Mr. Davidson, I am willing to be examined, but before this policy is paid for, I want to give every insurance company that has an office in any building I manage an opportunity to compete for the policy." That meant over fifty companies.

After I left, I said to myself, "He's not paying for this policy. He's not buying it. He is just presenting a life to be insured. The company that is paying for it should decide which insurance company will get it."

I placed this application with the Penn Mutual Life Insurance Company of Philadelphia. The morning after the client was examined in New York, the Penn Mutual representative, Mrs. Cecil Schultz, was at the Philadelphia office before its doors were opened and she managed to get the policy issued that day. This, of course, was very unusual. So the next day - two days after the examination - I called on the treasurer of the company which was paying for the insurance. The treasurer was a total stranger to me. After we had discussed the general qualifications of the Penn Mutual Company and the merits of the policy, I said, "Mr. H. told me that he intended to have each life insurance agency that was located in any of the buildings he managed present a competitive proposition and he wanted to hear from all of them before he bought." I let that sink in and then I asked, "Did you ever see a dog fight?"

He said, "Yes."

I said, "I mean one where a whole lot of dogs were all fighting."

He said, "Yes."

I said, "If they were all strange dogs, would you like to go in there and straighten them out?"

"No," he said, "I wouldn't."

"Well," I said, "that dog fight isn't anything compared to the fight there will be if these fifty life insurance agencies all get into a fight as to why each one should have this policy. You are paying for the policy. You have a perfect right to call in all of those fifty companies and get into the middle of the worst dog fight you ever saw in your life. And, as long as you are paying for it, you also have the privilege of asking someone in your office to write the check and hand the check to me. I will then hand the policy to you and the entire matter will be completed. It is just that simple. Which do you want to do?"

Well, although I was a total stranger, he gave me the check. Why? Because I used the power of suggestion and left the decision up to him. I described something that he was familiar with - a dog fight. And I told him the truth. A dog fight was nothing compared to the fight there would have been with fifty different life insurance agencies all trying to get that policy.

The suggestion got me the business and a substantial check on a $500,000 policy.

The next time you read the Bible, notice the frequency of the use of suggestion. The first sentence in Genesis is a direct positive statement. No reason is given. No proof is offered. It is suggestion. The last sentence in Revelation is also suggestion. One reason why the Bible has changed more lives than any other book is its frequent use of the power of suggestion.

~ CHAPTER 12 ~

MAKING POSITIVE USE OF THE NEGATIVE

AT THE BEGINNING of this book I promised you that I was not going to deal in theory. One reason is that theories change. A theory that seemed perfectly plausible ten years ago may be proved today to be perfectly ridiculous. There was once a theory upon which all experts in salesmanship were united. That was, "Never present the negative, always present the positive."

In this chapter, I propose to show you how actual experience tears that theory all to pieces. It never has been correct. It wasn't right when Solomon was teaching the principles of good business and salesmanship to the young men of his day, three thousand years ago. It wasn't right when Moses sold the children of Israel on the idea of getting out of Egypt, and then sold the king of Egypt on the idea of letting the great matrimonial sale that brought together Ruth and Boaz from whose union eventually came Jesus of Nazareth. It wasn't true when Jesus Himself sold twelve men on the idea of taking the message for which He had lived and died to every creature on the earth. It wasn't true when Paul stood on Mars Hill and sold some Athenian students of philosophy on the idea of accepting a God about whom they had never heard before, but whom they had been ignorantly worshipping.

When the excerpts told me that I must never mention the negative, that I must always present the positive, I went to my Book of master salesman to see what they had done. First I studied the man Moses. Moses was one of the greatest salesmen of ideas who ever lived. He went to a people who had been in slavery for centuries and sold them on the idea that they could arise, revolt, and escape their masters. Do you think that you would have been a good enough salesman to have gone down into the deep South after the slaves had been there for fifty years and sold them on the idea of revolt? Well, Moses did far more than that. He sold his idea to people who had been slaves for *four hundred* years.

They had to be completely and overwhelmingly dissatisfied with the position they were in before anyone could get them to think about changing. And, as little as we may have thought about it, that is one of the strongest points in salesmanship. When Mr. Kettering was active in the Engineering Department of General Motors, someone asked him one day what his job was. He replied, "My job is to make the American automobile owner dissatisfied with his present car." Moses did a piece of master salesmanship by making the slaves of Egypt completely and overwhelmingly dissatisfied with there situation. He did it by accenting the negative.

Thirty-five years ago, my superiors did not agree with that principle. They said to me, "Never present the negative. Don't get people dissatisfied. Just tell them how good it's going to be."

That is what I heard again and again. But my Book of master salesmen didn't agree with that at all. Moses, Jeremiah, Isaiah, Jonah, John the Baptist - men who changed the lives of thousands of people - sold their ideas by using the fear motive, by presenting the negative. They told those people unpleasant things, things that they didn't want to hear. And yet my bosses were saying to me, "Don't mention unpleasant things. Never back the hearse up to the door."

Who was right? Was the vice president in charge of sales of my company right? Were the advertising schools right? Were the experts in salesmanship right? Or were all of them wrong and the prophets right? Of course, the prophets were right.

"Oh, no!" someone will say. "They were all right in that day, but that was thousands of years ago. The situation is different today."

Applesauce! The basic principles of human relationships never change. That is one thing that we must fix firmly in our minds. Methods may change. Emphases may change. Products may change. The market may change. But the fundamental principles of salesmanship and good business never change one iota. What was right three thousand years ago is right today. That is what makes the Bible different from all other books of the world, whether those books are on religion, science, salesmanship, or any other subject. The Bible was right when it was first written and it is still right today. That is why anyone in this world with normal intelligence, and industry enough to apply himself to the task, can succeed by simply following the principles laid down in the Bible.

Of course it is now recognized in salesmanship and in advertising that the prophets' method was right. Today, a salesman selling electric typewriters will tell you that he can't go into an office and replace old-style typewriters with electric typewriters unless he first makes his prospects dissatisfied with the typewriters they already have. So it is generally recognized today that you want to sell something new, you must first dissatisfy the prospect with what he already has.

God told Jonah to go to the city of Nineveh, containing more than a million people, and tell them: "Yet forty days, and Nineveh shall be overthrown."

Jonah's message was entirely negative. If Jonah had been like some of the preachers and business experts of our day, he might have said, "Now, my good people, I don't want to say anything to disturb you or to hurt your feelings, but I believe that if you will make some changes in your manner of living you will find things a little more pleasant for you forty years from now."

What do you think would have happened? You are right - nothing. Here is what Jonah did say: "In forty days Nineveh shall be destroyed!"

And what happened when he used this fear motive - the negative method? He changed the thinking and the actions of the majority of the people in that city so that they repented, and the city was saved.

Now let me give you an example of how I used Jonah's method to sell an ambassador a million dollars' worth of life insurance. My wife and I were sitting in the railroad station in Chicago one day waiting to get a train to New York when suddenly over the loudspeaker I heard my name called. I answered a phone call and was told by my New York office that I was to go down to Bradsville that night to see the secretary of an important ambassador the next morning. They said, "She will give you all the information you need to prepare a plan for the Ambassador before he goes back to Europe."

I spent the next morning with the ambassador's secretary. She gave me all the information I requested., including copies of his tax returns, his will, the charter of his company, its balance sheet and income statements, etc. After getting all this data, I left on the one o'clock train for New York on Friday, and all the time I was on the train I was going through those statements trying to find everything that I could that looked negative. I was deliberately trying to find ways to worry the ambassador.

Saturday morning, I wrote him in Georgia where he was shooting quail. This is part of the letter I wrote: "It seems to me that if you should die without making any changes, there are some things that will happen that you don't want to happen." Then I listed some of those things. I wrote further, "A great many of these things can be corrected, and I shall be glad to discuss them with you before you go back to Europe."

The ambassador sent me a request to meet him in Washington on the morning of the day that he was sailing. He was to leave at midnight. When I met him, he pulled my letter out of his pocket, put it down on the piano, and said, "Davidson, that is the most terrible letter that any man ever wrote."

I said, "What's the trouble, Ambassador? Did I make some mistakes in it?"

"No," he said, "that's the worst part of it. It's all true. I am not exaggerating, I have not had a good night's sleep since I got the letter."

I told him that some of the things could be corrected and explained to him how buying a million dollars' worth of life insurance would help.

He said, "All right, we'll do that."

He told me that he had a luncheon engagement with President Roosevelt, and as he was going out to the elevator I said, "Ambassador, do you want to be examined for this insurance today?"

He said, "Yes, that won't take long, will it?"

I said truthfully, "Yes, it will. You will have to be examined separately by two doctors, you will have to have X rays made by another, and then you will have to have cardiograms made by another. It will take quite a bit of time."

"Well," he said, "after I see Mr. Roosevelt I have to see Cordell Hull - he's my boss, and I haven't seen him while I've been over here and I shouldn't go back to Europe without seeing him."

I looked him in the eye and said, "Ambassador, I know nothing about your duties to Mr. Roosevelt or to Mr. Hull, but I do know that as far as your family is concerned and as far as your wishes regarding your business after your death are concerned, there is nothing in the world as important to you as being examined here today."

He thought a minute or two and said, "I guess that's right."

He went over to the telephone, picked it up and broke his appointment with Cordell Hull.

Now here is the point I want to make. Suppose I had said in a namby-pamby way, "Now, Mr. Ambassador, I only want to talk to you about the pleasant things. I don't want to say anything that is unpleasant. I don't want to hurt your feelings. But if you go through with this life insurance program I think that everything will work out smoothly and it will be much nicer than it is now."

Do you think that on such reasoning as that he would have broken an appointment with the Secretary of State just to be examined for life insurance? He took the insurance, all of the changes suggested were made, and the things he desired have been accomplished. The point I want to make is that I couldn't have made that sale at all on the basis of just saying nice, pleasant things.

In the early part of this century, a man by the name of Lambert developed a mouthwash solution which he called "Listerine." Listerine never made much progress so fas as sales were concerned until after the death of Mr. Lambert. About 1925, Gerard Lambert, the son of Listerine's originator, came into control of the Lambert Company and started to put Listerine on the map. In doing so, he violated all the principles of advertising at that time. He used the method of the prophets. He coined the word "halitosis" and he insulted all of the American people by trying to make everyone afraid that his breath smelled bad. There was nothing positive about that kind of advertising or salesmanship!

But it has been estimated that by following the prophet's method, Gerard Lambert made between twenty and thirty million dollars. After the "halitosis" advertising campaign proved to be so successful, the advertising specialists changed their minds, started the "body odor" campaign, and racked their brains to find new ways of making the public afraid of everything.

Before a doctor operates, he puts on rubber gloves. When it is necessary for the doctor to cut here or to put clamp there, he is not dominated by emotions. But it was the emotion of fear that gave rubber gloves to surgery.

Many years ago, when the greatest hospital in the United States was the Massachusetts General Hospital in Boston, the most famous surgeon in that hospital was in love with a surgical nurse. At that time they didn't use iodine, iodoform, or Mercurochrome for antiseptic purposes. They used carbolic acid. The nurse had to keep the surgical instruments sterilized, and since the carbolic acid was coming in constant contact with her hands, her hands were literally being eaten up. She applied for a change of position. The surgeon couldn't imagine letting her leave. He wanted her to be with him in his work, to assist him and to work jointly with him. So, for fear of losing her companionship, he had to find a way to overcome the obstacle. He went to a man who dealt in rubber and said, "How about it? Could you make some gloves out of rubber?"

The man said, "I'll try."

So they made some gloves for the nurse, and she did not have to leave her physician-lover. She stayed right there as his assistant. And when they saw how wonderfully the gloves worked for her, it was just one more step for the rubber gloves to be used by the surgeon himself. That's what happened because a nurse was afraid of ruining her beautiful hands, and a surgeon was afraid of losing the nurse. Fear worked wonders!

After I began consciously to use this negative principle, I found that I should have been using it all the time, even in selling life insurance in small amounts. For instance, I had a chart which I had used very little - a picture of a hundred young men at age twenty-five, then showing them forty years later, at age sixty-five, with five of them being independent financially.

One way of using it would be to say: "Look, are you going to be one of the five who are independently financially when you are sixty-five? Wouldn't that be fine for you?"

The other way, and I believe it would have been the more effective way, would have been to picture the living conditions of the other ninety-five young men who would not be financially independent at the age of sixty-five. After I learned the Jonah method, I did use that chart in this way. I told my prospects about businessmen whose names were well known and who at sixty-five were penniless. Some had to live on relatives and some had to live on the county, and as I helped my prospects to visualize these cases, they would say, "I certainly don't want to be like that when I am sixty-five. I want to plan so as to be with the five independents."

Of course, that gave me the opportunity to present a plan of investment for the future through life insurance. The fear motive, I found, was more effective than just showing the happy side.

A three-month-old baby doesn't have much in its head that it has received from the teachings of its father and mother. But there is something inside that baby's head, and that is instinct which he gets from God. Without any teaching at all, that baby knows how to get the father up at two o'clock in the morning, no matter how sleepy Dad may be, or how much he wants to stay in bed. The baby knows how, and he doesn't do it by smiling or gurgling. But the baby wakes the father up. The father says, "Oh my! I've just got to sleep. It's two o'clock." Then he turns over to go back to sleep, but you know he doesn't. The baby wins out. He knows how to accentuate the negative!

~ CHAPTER 13 ~

THE FIGHTING FINISH

SOME YEARS AGO a group of life insurance salesmen asked me to tell how I handled the closing of one of the big cases on which I got a check for more than a million dollars. Of course, there is not set procedure. Each case is different and must be handled according to the circumstances of the moment.

Also, if every one of the obstacles is not overcome, the sale is lost and the commission simply does not materialize. In the second and third chapters of the Book of Revelation the angel repeats seven times that the rewards are to those who *overcome*. "He that *overcometh*... I will not blot out his name out of the book of life." "Him that *overcometh* will I make a pillar in the temple of my god." "To him that *overcometh* will I grant to sit with me in my throne, even as I also *overcame*, and am set down with my Father in his throne." The Apostle Paul said, "I have fought a good fight, I have kept the faith"; and that is what I want to be able to say at the close of each case I work on.

A good example of what I have been saying could be found in a case where the premium check was for $1,050,000. It is not by any means the largest sale I ever made, but it is typical of the last-minute difficulties to be encountered in this type of work.

A large single-premium endowment and annuity policy was to be sold to a family investment corporation. Seven men composed the board of directors. Each of these seven men had to be sold, one at a time. A firm of attorneys was counsel for this corporation. They had to be sold, too - so thoroughly sold that they would back the plan with their written legal opinion. A firm of nationally known accountants were tax consultants for this group. They had to be convinced that every tax angle (income, inheritance, and estate) of the plan was sound - and they had to back up their acquiescence with a written opinion. Still another firm of auditors were the operating accountants for this holding corporation. They had to be sold the plan from a fact-and-figure angle so that they would approve it in writing. All this was accomplished.

"Now," said the president of the corporation, "we will have a special meeting of the board." The meeting was called. The attorney and the seven board members were there - and a new face, too - a stock exchange house representative who was not a member of the board but who had been invited to attend as an advisor. I sat in the meeting to answer questions.

The stock exchange member started the party with an objection. "There is no assurance that the dividends on this policy will be continued at the present rate," he objected.

"We know that," replied the two chief men at interest. "Mr. Davidson has explained that possibility and has even suggested that we forecast our results on the basis of dividend returns being only 50 per cent as great as the company is now paying. Even on that basis this plan is the best we have found."

Previously I have emphasized the value of absolute truthfulness and the fact that *understatement* has a power all its own. This case was an excellent illustration of what I meant. Instead of exaggerating the probable amount of the dividends, I had not only slated the present dividend rate accurately, but I had also deliberately *understated* my belief in the future dividend possibilities. Now, when the critical moment arrived, this served me in good stead. Had I previously overstated, my sale would have been lost right there.

Round the table the objections flew. Each had his say, including the attorney. Finally they excused me. "We will talk this over privately - you wait outside." After a painful wait, the group filed out; apparently all matters in connection with the purchase had been satisfactorily settled. The attorney put on his hat to leave: "I find no further points to discuss here. Everything seems in order. [Here my spirits rose to a high point.] But before you issue this check for $1,050,000, I recommend that you have your auditing firm examine the policies themselves, verify all the figures, and give you their approval in writing."

I had left as little as possible to chance. I always try to think of every obstacle in advance and to be prepared for it. Of course, this takes thought and planning. It requires some imagination to project yourself into the various future situations which may arise. I had foreseen that the clients in this case would require the auditors' written verification of the figures, and had already placed the policies in the auditors' hands with a request that they be examined and approved well in advance. When the attorney made this request, I merely asked that the auditors be phoned and their written verification be sent to my clients' office.

The fear of buying is very great when a man is writing a check for more than a million dollars. He is afraid of this own judgement - afraid that some little mistake, some tiny oversight, may cost him heavily. Hence he is often reluctant to part with the check even after he has agreed to go through with the deal.

While my clients were out to lunch I personally went to the auditors' office, saw to it that a proper letter of verification was prepared, and personally accompanied one of the auditors back to my clients' office. I took no chances on anything happening in between. But when the auditors' verification was in hand and the order to issue the check seemed no longer subject to delay, the treasurer pointed out that they couldn't issue the check that day anyway as they did not have that much money in the bank.

"Where is the money?" I asked.

"In two brokerage houses. We will have to withdraw about a half million from each, and we can't hope to get that today. Besides, one of the houses is a small one and they will probably have to sell securities to realize the cash. That will have to be done tomorrow."

It happened that this brokerage house employed the son of the holding corporation's president. The son was present. Turning to him, I inquired: "Why, a half million dollars will not mean anything to a firm like yours, will it?"

And the young man, proud of his firm, replied, "Certainly not. I'll call them right now and see if they can accommodate us."

"To be sure," said the brokerage partner at the other end of the line, "you can have our certified check for a half a million within thirty minutes if you wish."

"And there is no question about the other house on the second half million?" I asked.

"No," my clients admitted, "they can give us a check any time."

Once again it seemed as if every hurdle had been topped and every possible objection overcome.

But the secretary thought hard. "Well, even if we get these brokerage house checks we can't give you ours. You want it certified, don't you? We have to deposit them in our bank in Wilmington and get our check to you certified after that. It will be impossible under any circumstances to do that today."

This happened to be Friday afternoon. If I did not get the checks then, I could not see them again until Monday afternoon - seventy two hours. I said: "No need to go through all that red tape. Just have the brokerage houses make out their checks to your corporation, each check being for the amount due on each policy, and have them certified. Then you endorse them to the insurance companies and we will hand them over and give you their receipts."

This was agreed to.

"Have you the receipts?" they asked.

"Some of them," I replied, "but certain of the companies will not issue a receipt on a large policy until the remittance is in the hands of their agency cashier."

"Well, of course, we can't hand you these checks until you can hand us the receipts."

"I have arranged for that," I rejoined. "Two agency cashiers are on the way here at this moment. When they arrive, they will hand you the receipts and accept these certified checks."

My clients' ingenuity was exhausted. The group could think of no more hurdles. The cashiers arrived, the checks were paid over and receipts delivered. I took home with me, and kept at home over the weekend, checks totaling over a million dollars, and I went home that night almost $40,000 richer than when I ate breakfast that morning.

~ CHAPTER 14 ~

CAN THE ORDINARY PERSON SUCCEED?

LET'S FACE IT, Some people seem to get all the favorable "breaks" while a good many others tempt us to think that perhaps Mohammed was right in teaching that some persons are destined for heaven, some for hell, some for fortune and some for misery - and that no one can change his fate by an inch. As you have read this book you may have been asking, "What about the ordinary fellow like me? In spite of all your claims to the contrary, Clinton Davidson, I have a hunch that you must have a lot of special ability to swing those million-dollar deals you have told about. Not every private becomes a general. Do you really think that ordinary people can reach success?"

My friend, *I am one of those ordinary fellows myself.* I never received a high school or college diploma. I have spent years at the very bottom of the financial heap, wondering wearily whether I could ever rise as high as the majority of my acquaintances. I know how if feels to come home at night dead tired, to worry about the future, to wonder whether you will ever get anywhere in life. When I say that anyone can use the principles in the Bible to rise high, I know what I'm talking about, for no one could have had a lower start than I had.

And I had an extra handicap - or what seemed like a handicap - from my religious training. I couldn't drink, gamble, or sit up at night "carousing" with my clients. I was not accepted easily as "one of the boys." For this reason I often said to myself, "Clint, two or three hundred dollars a month is going to be the top for you in this business - you might as well face it."

Yes, I passed through a period when all my thinking was small and I was very discouraged by the hard facts of life. But as the principles of success I found in the Bible became a part of my work, here is what happened.

I went back to my office on Saturday afternoons when no one else was there and thought. I had those familiar surroundings all to myself on those quiet afternoons and I sat at my desk trying to pierce the veil of the future. I looked and planned ahead as far as I could see, and at times I even put an experimental foot forward into territory I couldn't see. And ideas began to come. One Saturday afternoon during the war years, it flashed across my mind that there should be come way to take advantage of a good habit that had been impressed on everyone during the war. The whole nation had been told to save money and put it into war saving stamps, liberty bonds, and the like.

I had been reading somewhere that one week in the year was to be known as National Thrift Week. I inquired at the insurance agents' association, the savings banks, and the local clearing house, but no one knew anything about it. Finally I wrote to the headquarters of the Thrift Society to get the information. Thrift, they told me, included saving, buying homes, life insurance, etc. It seemed that this was an idea to which I might profitably tie up, so I went to the main office of the L & N Railroad, which was located in Louisville, where I was working. They had 2,000 clerks working in one large building. Picking out one of the largest departments, I went to the chief clerk with this story:

"Thrifty men and women make better employees than spenders, don't they?"

"Yes!" he answered.

"As head of this office, you are naturally interested in having the best type of employees possible, are you not?"

Of course, he agreed that he was.

Then I told him the story of National Thrift Week and explained that I was prepared to address his employees during the last fifteen minutes of their lunch-hour period, if he would announce the meeting the day before. He agreed to this. I insisted beforehand that no employee be compelled to attend. Nevertheless, about half the office force attended. I secured from an insurance magazine some large charts explaining life insurance as a form of property, and, standing on a chair, I made my talk. We offered miniature copies of the charts free, if the listeners would place their names and addresses on plain white cards which we supplied. Many of them asked for the miniature charts.

The first meeting was so successful that it was easy to sell other chief clerks the idea. Soon, they offered to hold the meeting on company time, not employees' time. When the campaign of talks was completed, we had secured over 500 requests for the charts and sold many of the clerks policies of $1,000 and $2,000 each.

Eventually the National Association of Life Underwriters took part in National Thrift Week, their activities increasing from year to year until finally it became Life Insurance Week, not Thrift Week. Approximately $1,000,000 has been spent to promote it. But on that Saturday afternoon, when in my planning hour I first thought of tying up Thrift Week, no one in Louisville had ever thought of having a national week for life insurance. Doesn't it seem reasonable to suppose that if someone else had had a planning hour, the idea of tying into Thrift Week would have come to him as easily as to me?

Later on I attended a night law school where I studied about wills, trusts, and the administration of estates. Life insurance was only *one* of the instruments by means of which a man distributes his property at death, and if I was going to talk about one, I wished to be able to talk intelligently about the others. I wasn't selling mere insurance anyway. I was selling a plan to fit the other man's estate needs, and to make and sell such plans, I needed to know about wills, trusts, holding corporations, etc. Anybody can do now, or could have done then, what I did. Most of them don't do it, perhaps because they prefer watching television.

When I moved up the scale a little and got into slightly larger cases where expert advice was needed, I hired the best tax accountants and the best estate lawyer I could find, and paid them their fees to work out the details of plans for my prospective clients. In every department of my work I was endeavoring to prepare myself to render superlative service. Those who were trying to compete with me in my type of selling were not willing to pay lawyers and tax accountants for their advice and assistance. If it could be gotten free, or if the client could be made to pay for it out of his own pocket, he got it. But my competition never followed me in this expensive plan of giving my clients and prospects the best personal estate service of its kind that could be had.

Another thing I found very helpful was spending long hours in the surrogate's office, studying the wills of the leading families of the city, filed for probate. Here were the confidential plans of the leading wealthy men of the city laid open before me to study. Here was to be found the crystalized thinking of the most astute businessmen of the community. Here were no dead and dusty theories, but the living plans conceived by leading attorneys for our foremost citizens.

This study did several things for me. It gave me a valuable hindsight view of the estate plans of these able men, showing me the plans which had failed and those which had succeeded. It also gave me an almost endless array of living examples of actual mistakes and oversights which I could use in my selling. And they were mistakes and oversights of the men and women whom our prospects knew, or knew about. My sales talk, when composed of this material, proved resistibly interesting!

These things were all groundwork. They made the foundation on which the remainder of the accomplishments, such as it is, could be built. I don't believe the accomplishment would have been possible without the foundation, and I don't believe the laying of the foundation required any education, determination, effort, or sacrifice not possible for anyone to make.

When I learned of a prospect who was going to move into a new office, I promptly reported it to one of my customers who was in the office furniture and supply business. When I found a man in the market for a motor car or truck, I got in touch with one of my customers who had such items for sale, and gave him the tip. I didn't do this merely for prospects, but I did it for customers - people whose money I had already collected and probably spent. I did it as part of the friendly, helpful *service* that I was resolved to render.

The same principle still works. Twenty years ago, I had sold a distinguished member of the Du Poet family a large policy and received a check for considerably more than $1,000,000. I called on this man at his office and suggested that certain of my associates were in the position to give certain of his associates quite a little volume of financial business, and I wished to discuss with them the best method of doing so. He knew that I had nothing to sell him; he had been sold and the money was paid. He looked at me a moment and remarked, "You know, Mr. Davidson, in thirty-five years I think this is the first time that anybody who has sold me anything has offered voluntarily to do something for me." Because he was an extremely wealthy man, everybody had been busy trying to get part of his wealth away from him instead of trying to help him. This client appreciated my offer of service probably more than any client I could recall.

The second or third man whom I sold when I was starting to work out the Estate Planning method was Mr. Pardee of Buffalo, New York, who was high in the Spirella Corset Company of Niagara Falls. This large and very profitable corporation had offices in many countries and at that time had a sales force of some 15,000 people. I know of no other manufacturing company that had a sales force this large. He purchased $750,000 of insurance, and this was my second largest sale at that time. Mr. Pardee came to have considerable confidence in my business judgement and came to me with many financial problems.

Later on, after I moved to New York City, he called me one day saying that he was considering the creation of a corporation in Canada to hold his Canadian investments, and he very much wanted to discuss the matter with me. I came from New York to Buffalo at my own expense. Of course, I felt complimented that he desired to initiate the subject with me instead of with his attorney, but I didn't overlook the fact that in addition to the transportation and hotel costs this would take several days out of the difficult period I was going through in trying to get established in New York City. In discussing the subject with Mr. Pardee and his attorney, I suggested what I thought was an original idea, the use of a corporation for one of his purposes that issued common stock payable to bearer. Mr. Pardee was intrigued with the idea. (Later, I learned that the idea was not original, but had been used previously by some very large corporations.) Before I left Buffalo, Mr. Pardee said, "Clinton, I have been talking to some friends about your services and they have become interested. I should like to make an appointment for you to see them." So, although my trip to Buffalo was made solely for the purpose of rendering service, the service, as usual, resulted in an unexpected profit.

Later on, I secured as a prospect the late William S. Farish, then president of the Standard Oil Company of New Jersey. I suggested that Mr. Farish purchase half a million dollars of insurance on the life of his son and the same amount on the life of his daughter. This was done. When I secured the application for his son, I learned that he had taken lessons flying while a student at Yale, and, if I remember correctly, had previously owned his own plane. In those days it was very difficult for one who piloted his own plane to get unrestricted life insurance. A policy was usually offered which did not insure against death resulting directly from flying. In some cases the policies permitted flying on commercial lines, but not otherwise. My applicant said that he no longer owned a plane, that he had not piloted a plane since leaving college, that he was now firmly established in business and had no desire to be an amateur pilot, his license had lapsed, and, furthermore, he had promised his wife that he would not do any piloting int he future.

Because he felt so certain that the insurance could not be issued without a clause which excluded death resulting from flying planes without a clause which excluded death resulting from flying planes other than those on commercial air lines, he said he would not object to a policy containing this clause. However, I felt that as a matter of service to him I should make every effort to secure $500,000 of life insurance policies which contained no aviation restrictions whatsoever. I could have secured the restricted policies with no more effort on my part than that of mailing him the application. It took me several weeks to secure the unrestricted policies. I submitted an application first to only one company, the company that had the most liberal experience in this respect. After that policy was issued, I sent a photostat of it to the second most liberal company. After that was issued, I sent photostats of both policies to several other companies, and, as a result of telephone and personal calls, the entire $500,000 was issued without restrictions.

This principle of service is the heart and lifeblood of selling. It is not complicated. It is very simple; anybody can understand it. The first step is to be qualified in your own line, to know how to apply what you are selling to your prospect's needs. Then, study to make yourself an authority both on your product or service and on the needs of people who might profit from your help.

I needed to know all I could learn about life insurance. Many men knew that; but I also needed to know all I could about how men could *use* life insurance to solve their personal estate problems. That meant that I had to know these problems. And know them I did, although this took several years of study late at night.

If I were selling electric refrigerators, I would become an authority on food preservation, on the preparation of frozen desserts and chilled salads. I would understand the principle of keeping children's milk fresh and preventing illness. I would stop in and see my buyers once in a while and leave them a new recipe, or give them a helpful household hint. Whatever else was required of me I would certainly carry out the principle of service in selling refrigerators. Yet, I am told by a man in that business that only one salesman in a hundred can be induced to call back on a customer once he has gotten her order. How shortsighted can salesmen be!

To sum up, I don't believe anyone is destined to remain mediocre. If he has no education, he can get it - much more easily today that I could get it years ago. If he doesn't know this business, he can learn it. If he doesn't know this prospects and their needs, he can find out about them by a little persistent effort.

You can say with the Apostle Paul, "I can do all things through Christ which strengtheneth me!" And you can make that true in your own experience. That I know, for I am one of the ordinary persons who did it.

~ CHAPTER 15 ~

DISCOVER YOUR OWN SUCCESS SECRETS

EVERY PAGE IN the Bible is a success page. From beginning to end it warns of dangers of failure, inspires to victory, and assures that God's great plan for a world of peace and blessing is going to succeed. The primary purpose of the Bible, of course, is to bring men and women spiritual and moral success, to equip us for everlasting life with God. However, He has much more to offer us than what one cynic called "Pie in the sky bye and bye." God's way is right not only for spiritual victories and future blessings but for making the best of life here and now. What the Bible says of the men and women who walk through its pages shows the weaknesses that led to their downfall, and also the resources by which they triumphed over every kind of obstacle. And the greatest men and women of the past two thousand years have been nurtured and inspired by this Book which has no equal.

It must be obvious that what I have said thus far about the techniques of success I found in the Bible has barely scratched the surface. This book was written in the hope that many readers will turn from it to the Book of books and there discover new principles of success, not only for achievement in this world but for the final satisfaction of hearing the words: "Well done, thou good and faithful servant: thou has been faithful over a few things, I will make thee ruler over many things: enter thou into the joy of thy Lord" (Matthew 25:21).

I would urge anyone who wants to find his own success secrets in the Bible to pay special attention to what is said about the men and women it presents. I have referred to a few of them and to what they can teach us about success. There are many hundreds more. You will find them in almost every book in the Bible. Nothing is held back, nothing covered up. The sin and folly of each one is laid out alongside his faith and wisdom. James tells us that Elijah was a man "subject to like passions as we are" (5:17) - but he turned a whole nation away from a pagan queen and her heathen gods to serve the true Lord. And the same Power available to Elijah is available today.

Consider the Book of Proverbs. There you will find outlined all of the principles of business success in all the books of the last fifty years. Those principles were there all the time, discovered and practiced by such men as Benjamin Franklin and Marshall Field, but largely unknown to many people. One businessman, however, always carried small paper-covered copies of Proverbs in his pocket, read them at odd moments, and gave them away.

Here is one example of what you will find in Proverbs: "It is naught, it is naught, saith the buyer: but when he is gone his way, then he boasters" (20:14). What does this mean? That when you are trying to sell something you should not be cowed or defeated because your prospective customer throws up a strong front of sales resistance. It is human nature for him to "talk down" what he wants at the same time that he is really looking forward to having it. Understanding this can make the sale easier.

Another example of the gems you will discover as you mine the treasure-laden contents of the Bible for yourself is in the first nine verses of the First Chapter of Joshua. There we can see Joshua, the younger understudy of Moses, in dismay after Moses' death. He has to make Moses' place in leading the Children of Israel into the Promised Land - and in wrestling that land from the hordes of savages who already possess it. he is the only leader left. He has to become the President, Congress, Supreme Court, and Joint Chiefs of Staff all in one in waging one of the most difficult wars ever fought.

What does the Lord tell Joshua? "Every place that the sole of your foot shall tread upon, that have I given you." That is a promise that you can apply to the paths you travel today - if you fulfill the conditions that follow.

"Be strong and of a good courage... do according to all the law, which Moses my servant commanded thee: turn not from it to the right hand or to the left, that thou mayest prosper whithersoever thou goest. This book of the law shall not depart out of they mouth; but thou shalt meditate therein day and night, that thou mayest observe to do according to all that is written therein: for then thou shalt make thy way prosperous, and then thou shalt have good success."

This is God's own promise of success.

I believe that you can find within the covers of the Bible wisdom to meet every kind of situation. One of my associates told me one day that he had been invited to address a group of bankers at an important meeting on the subject of trusteeship, and wanted my help.

"Why come to me?" I asked. "I've never turned the world upside down with any of my speeches. Why not go to the Apostle Paul? He did turn the world upside down and I believe he was the most effective speaker in all time. Why don't you use the outline he used in ! Corinthians 13?"

There Paul lists the things highly esteemed by his readers: eloquent speech, the gift of prophecy, faith, and works of charity. All these are nothing, he says, unless you also have love. Then he tells what love is. Finally, he shows why it is the greatest thing in the world.

I said to my associate, "Why don't you follow exactly the same outline in your address on trusteeship? Begin as Paul began, enumerating the things your banker listeners hold in highest esteem, such as the value of banking, the importance of securities, the necessity for the brokerage business, and so on. Then show that a man may seem to be a success in all these things, but if he lacks the inherent quality of trusteeship he fails in the most important qualification of all for a banker. Name some of the brilliant men who have failed as bankers simply because they lacked trusteeship. Then analyze trusteeship: explain what it is and what it means. Show its historical background, its ethical foundations, its responsibilities and opportunities. Make your hearers understand trusteeship not only intellectually but also emotionally, with their hearts. Close by showing why the true quality of trusteeship is the greatest thing in the business of banking: the highest concept of business and banking ethics. Do these three things and those bankers will never forget what you say."

My friend took Paul's outline and built his speech on it, and it was the most effective address in his career.

You can find in the Bible not only the wisdom of the ages, accepted by the great faiths, but the message of God to you. When you go to the Bible you will find God's counsel. In the first hour's reading you may not find the solution to all your problems, but if you continue to read you will hear God speaking to you, and if you obey His voice you will find your problems straightening themselves out, one by one.

Many people prefer the King James Version of the Bible. Others find that many passages are clearer in one of the recent translations in modern English. Whatever version of the Bible you have, read it and hear for yourself the Word of God.

Here is one of the great assurances of the Bible:

Blessed is the man that walketh not in the counsel of the ungodly, nor standeth in the way of sinners, nor sitters in the seat of the scornful. But his delight is in the law of the Lord; and in his law doth he meditate day and night. And he shall be like a three planted by the rivers of water, that bringeth forth his fruit in his season; his leaf also shall not wither; and whatsoever he doth shall prosper.

This is what God Himself says in the First Psalm. Look up to Him in faith, meditate on His law of blessing in the Bible, be diligent in whatsoever you do, and you shall prosper.

ACKNOWLEDGEMENTS

Mr. Burton Bigelow, who is without equal as an adviser in sales management and planning, served as my adviser and provided many of the ideas described in this book. Mr. G. H. Montgomery and Mr. Donald R. Kauffman greatly improved the manuscript that I prepared.

SCRAPBOOK & PHOTOS

"A Portrait of the Davidsons"
(Courtesy of the Davidson Family)

The Davidson Family
(Flora, Clinton & Clinton Davidson Jr.) c. 1920

The Davidson family originally lived in Louisville, Kentucky. Clinton Davidson's grandfather, Benjamin Franklin Davidson, served in the Union Army during the Civil War as an assistant surgeon. Clinton's father, Daniel Davidson became an orphan early in life before ending his own life tragically in 1891. Flora Davidson lost her mother during childbirth in 1895. Her father, Julius A. Schlueter was a hardware store owner from Louisville Kentucky. He came to live with the Davidsons at Balbrook after retiring in 1932. He built a rugged frontier log cabin on the estate without the use of nails that still stands today. He lived to be 82. Clinton Davidson's sister, Mary Davidson, married into the Rutherford family. One of her sons, Clinton Rutherford, became a minister for the Wildwood Church of Christ and also lived in a home on the Balbrook estate.

A Portrait of the Davidsons

Acquired and renovated during the Great Depression of the 1930's, Balbrook was originally a 250 acre estate located approximately 40 miles from New York City in the towns of Mendham and Bernardsville in New Jersey. It served as the home of Clinton and Flora Davidson, their son "Jack," grand children and great grand children until it was sold in 1981.

A strong supporter of the values of Christian education, Clinton made many financial contributions to Christian colleges. He helped save Harding College from fiscal mismanagement in the 1930's and gave speeches at Abilene Christian College in Texas. He helped establish Northeastern Christian Junior College near Villanova in Pennsylvania which later merged with Ohio Valley College in Vienna, West Virginia in 1993. He also sponsored the college educations of approximately 18 friends and family members. Many wealthy and influential business clients would visit the Davidson's estate. (below)

The "Little Church in the Wildwood" c. 1940

On the Balbrook property, Clinton and Flora started "The Little Church in the Wildwood" in a chapel built by the original owners, the Balbachs. The little chapel had a secret chamber in the cellar that was discovered when a furnace accidentally exploded to reveal an expensive Italian marble fireplace and a crypt with two empty stone coffins, presumably for the Balbachs children. The Wildwood Church of Christ congregation grew ever larger and eventually migrated to the church built at Shiloh.

A replica of a Bavarian chapel located in Germany that was constructed by the previous owner of Balbrook, the Balbachs. It is now perfectly restored after it had suffered some neglect and vandalism between property owners.

The Davidsons had four grandchildren and five great grand-children. Clinton Franklin Davidson III ("Frank") is above on the left and Adeline Sinclair Davidson ("Addie") is on the right and Clinton Davidson is center. Their granddaughter Flora (below) was only three years old when she died of a spinal meningitis infection. She is held here by her great grandfather, Julius A. Schlueter.

The Davidsons enjoyed travel. They journeyed to Cuba, Mexico, Europe, South America, Hawaii, California, Canada and many other places. Clinton Davidson was an outdoorsman and an avid swimmer.

A Portrait of the Davidsons

Flora Davidson with her good friend movie actress Loretta Young in Hawaii in the 1950's. Pat Boone is pictured below with Steve Davidson and Joyce Conroy at a picnic at the Balbrook lake in 1958.

A Portrait of the Davidsons

The Davidsons flying Imperial Airways of London. (Above)

(Left) Clinton's business partner, Raymond Hartz in Alberta, Canada with Flora Davidson. Raymond was a close friend and business partner with the Davidsons. (Below) Raymond Hartz, Flora Davidson's father, Julius A. Schlueter and Clinton Davidson vacationing in the 1920's.

Clinton Davidson, Jr. ("Jack")

Clinton and Flora's only child, Jack Davidson excelled at mathematics. After graduating from high school a year early, he was accepted at both Harvard and Yale. Yale would not accept students under 18 years of age at the time. Therefore, Jack attended Harvard for a year and then transferred to Yale where he earned his college degree. He taught economics as a professor at Harding University. After working for his father at Fiduciary Counsel, Inc. on Wall Street, he became the CEO of Washington based Resort Airlines, the largest private sector carrier of military cargo in the 1950's. Resort Airlines also provided tourist excursions to Cuba, Haiti and the Dominican Republic. He successfully brought the troubled airline back to profitability before suffering a fatal heart attack at the age of 46. Jack also was a preacher for Sunday services at The Little Church in the Wildwood. In the photo above, he's with his first wife, Kathryn Isabel Davidson ("K.I"), the daughter of Mr. and Mrs. John E. L. Davis of New York. They had three children together, Clinton Franklin Davidson III, Adeline Sinclair Davidson and baby Flora. Jack had another son, Steve Davidson (pictured on the previous page) with his second wife, Rosamond Davidson. At various times, the Balbrook estate was home to horses, cattle, hogs, chickens, dogs, cats, deer and many other animals and pets.

The Shiloh Mansion & Camp Shiloh

A Portrait of the Davidsons

Acquired in 1951 with financial help from the Davidsons and bordering the Balbrook estate, the Shiloh Mansion, once called 'Oakdene' and previously owned by the family who had owned Proctor & Gamble, was a thirty-six room fifty-three acre property and became the home of Camp Shiloh and the Wildwood Church of Christ. It served inner city youth from New York City. The building burned down during renovation work but was later restored to its original design.

The Camp Shiloh bus, 'The Grey Ghost,' would rescue kids from the inner city streets and bring them to the woods and countryside of Mendham each summer where they would enjoy swimming and outdoor activities at the lake at Balbrook. Clinton Davidson's nephew, Clinton Rutherford, a minister of the Wildwood Church of Christ, helped run the program with Eddie Grindley who had been a superintendent of an orphan's home in Arkansas where he met Clinton Davidson, Jr. Eager and idealistic college students were recruited from campuses across the country to 'give a year' for the children of Shiloh. They lived on no more than $150 a month, intentionally equivalent to the income of a family on welfare, an amount which they raised themselves from families, friends, and churches. The first inner city program began in 1967 with nine staff members living at Shiloh and commuting to inner city neighborhoods. Their numbers expanded to thirty-six in 1968 with the counselors living in the inner city neighborhoods with the children they served. Their numbers expanded to sixty-six in 1969, eighty in 1970. By the mid-70's there was a full-time, year-round staff of almost 100. In 1976, Camp Shiloh relocated outside of Woodbridge, N.Y. due to problems with residential zoning regulations enacted by the state of New Jersey. [1]

---

[1] See ShilohNYC: www.shilohnyc.org

History

Emil Menes, Jr. holds Rebecca Ann Menes, a great granddaughter of Clinton & Flora Davidson (c. 1962). Emil's father, Emil Menes, Sr. maintained the gardens at Balbrook and rented a home on the estate. The Menes family (Ménés) migrated permanently from Hungary to New Jersey in 1956. Other homes on the estate were rented to African-American families, a family from Mexico, the Garcia Family and the Clark family. The Clarks rented a colonial period home dating back before the Revolutionary War that the Davidsons had restored. Jackson Simmons, originally from Atlanta, Georgia, worked and lived as the Davidson's butler and chauffeur for over four decades on the estate. Nathan Carter, a minister and carpenter, and his wife Rose Carter also worked for the Davidsons at Balbrook. Clinton Davidson helped Nathan Carter purchase a building and establish a church in Trenton, New Jersey. During these years, Jackson Simmons also established a church in Morristown, New Jersey with Clinton Davidson's support. Below is the stone at the gate on Bernardsville Road that was placed by the previous owners of Balbrook, the Balbachs, in 1894.

Colonial Home

An Indian deed from 1708 was found in the colonial period home. Balbrook had once been called *Macksetacohunge* where an Indian village named *Peapock* once flourished. The Minisink Indians, one of the Algonquin tribes, lived on the stream they called *Hopkonocasey*. The entire area was purchased for thirty pounds in cash, thirty blankets of various kinds, fifteen kettles, twenty axes, half a barrel of wine, a barrel of rum, two barrels of cider, three files, four pistols, ten guns, a hundred bars of lead, half a barrel of powder, twenty shirts and one hundred knives. When the estate was sold after the passing of Flora Davidson, the historic home was demolished by developers after Reverend James A. Clark struggled to have it preserved or moved to another property. The colonial home was estimated to be one of the two oldest structures in the town of Mendham.

Frontier Cabin

In the 1930's, Julius A. Schlueter, Flora Davidson's father, who had previously owned a hardware store in Louisville, Kentucky, constructed this frontier log cabin. It was built with the techniques that were used in Kentucky during the frontier days without the use of nails or power tools. The cabin has stood for over 80 years next to the lake at Balbrook.

(Photos courtesy of the Davidson family.)

Pat Boone, Flora Davidson and Clinton Davidson

From the movie set of *Journey to the Center of the Earth*,
Los Angeles, CA. c. 1959

Pat Boone became a client and close friend of the Davidsons. Pat attended Lipscomb University in Nashville, Tennessee with the Davidson's granddaughter, Adeline Sinclair Davidson in 1952 in their senior year of high school. Afterwards, Pat went to Columbia University in New York City. The family, while watching Pat's half-hour variety tv show, *The Pat Boone Chevy Showroom* sparked Clinton Davidson's curiosity in the rising star and in 1957 quickly contacted Pat Boone concerning his wealth management services. Afterwards, the Boones, who lived in New Jersey at the time, would have picnics with the Davidsons at their estate. In 1959, Clinton Davidson and Pat Boone contributed generously to purchase the Morris Clothier estate and start a new Christian college in Villanova, Pennsylvania named Northeastern Christian Junior College.

A Portrait of the Davidsons

The Davidson Family Crest and the Davidson Coat of Arms, from Scotland, was on display at Balbrook. Proud of his Scottish heritage, Clinton knew the history of the Davidsons in America back to the Revolutionary War. Many settled in North Carolina where the British had described them as 'A hornests' nest of rebels.' The Davidson Clan fled religious persecution in Scotland and were expelled from England and sent to the American colonies, Australia, New Zealand and Canada. The Davidsons originated in the highlands with their history preserved today at the clan's Tulloch Castle in Scotland.

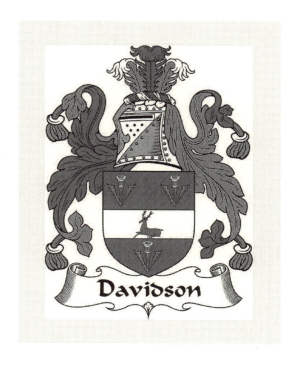

THIS WEEK in Washington

A column carried by over 900 newspapers in the 1950's, *THIS WEEK in Washington* covered politics, economics, agriculture and other topics. In 1958, Clinton wrote the following article about Pat Boone while on a trip to Los Angeles.

November 20, 1958

Pat Boone

I'm no teen-ager by almost half a century, but I've just spent one of the most enlightening and enjoyable days I can remember with the idol of millions of young folks.

The pleasant, energetic and tireless young man is, of course, Pat Boone. I had a special reason for wanting to spend a typical work day with Pat.

In Washington I have heard many discussions on what to do to reduce juvenile delinquency. There have been many conferences by educators, social workers and law enforcement officials on the subject.

The usual complaint was that young folks lack ambition and willingness to do hard work. Youth, they said, is lacking in the strong moral qualities upon which our forefathers built this nation. I don't believe it.

A Good Example

More young people admire Pat Boone than perhaps any other person living. I wanted to know what the qualities in him were that attracted so many young enthusiasts, to find out what he really is like.

His television show is No. 1 among all half-hour musical programs. He has maidenly three movies in two years, but he ranks No. 3 in movie box office attractions. He is estimated to have an audience of 23 million on TV alone.

Pat's day at 20th Century-Fox began at 8 AM, making a movie called "Mardi Gras." The scene was a park in New Orleans. Ten little colored children, each with a musical instrument, were in a cart pulled by a donkey. This formed the orchestra.

Pat sang a song and as he danced, he fell backwards over a small hedge. The day was hot; the donkey was stubborn; the children were difficult to control, and the scene had to be taken and retaken from 8 AM until 3 PM.

Music Maker

At a time of day when most business men are headed for home or the golf course, Pat dashed from the movie scene to a sound stage to record musical numbers until 6 PM.

He arrived home at 6:30 and an hour later he was at the Dot Recording Studios to record some new songs. At the end of two hours the first song had been recorded seventeen times.

The director, Randy Woods, who is President of Dot Records, Inc., was difficult to satisfy. Finally, at 9:30 PM, he said he would use the first half of the 11th recording and the last half of the 17th. Pat continued to work on other recordings until 11:30.

I doubt if any adult in the Untied States who criticize present-day young people works as hard as Pat. He held down three full-time jobs while attending Columbia University and still graduated among the top 5% of his class. He has continued his studies here in Hollywood.

If you want to encourage and inspire any young people, you cannot do it better than by suggesting that they emulate Pat Boone.

A Portrait of the Davidsons

An article touching on the need for nation-wide racial reconciliation after the 'Little Rock Nine' incident in Little Rock in 1957. The Davidsons helped establish African American Churches of Christ in Trenton and in Morristown, New Jersey by lending support to two of their long term employees at Balbrook, Nathan Carter and Jackson Simmons.

October 17, 1957

Little Rock is a Trigger

Little Rock is a trigger that, if pulled by the finger of hate could blow the brains out of our democracy.

A great deal of damage already has been done to our democratic processes. Old wounds that should have healed long ago have been reopened and undoubtedly will be slow to heal.

As a Southerner by birth (Atlanta) and rearing, I think I understand the feelings of the South. And as a resident of the North for many years, I know something of the people of that area.

I know that the loyalties of both are dedicated to the preservation of our Union and our democracy. There is a critical need now that we all think and act as Americans, not as Northerners or Southerners, not as segregationists or integrationists.

This is a critical time in our history. It is not time for chips on shoulders. There are many issues, but the all-important one is that we think and act reasonably, as Americans.

There needs to be a cooling-off period, a time in which to think and act reasonably and rationally, lest we precipitate, at the very least, a cold war between the states of our Nation.

The issues involve fundamental principles of our enduring democracy. We should face them and attempt to resolve them. They will not be ignored and they cannot be settled by attempting to fix blame for what has happened.

The Supreme Court unanimously ruled in 1954 that segregation of the races in schools is unconstitutional. The ruling was a judicial interpretation of the 14th Amendment.

Arkansas Governor Faubus challenged the right of the Federal government to enforce the decision in Little Rock Central High School. He used state troops to thwart a school board integration order.

When state troops were withdrawn at the urging of President Eisenhower, city police were unable to prevent rioting. Mr. Eisenhower ordered Federal troops to restore order and carry out Federal court integration order.

It is not my purpose here to argue either the necessity or legality of any of those three actions which precipitated, but did not create, the inflammatory issues involved.

My point is that the Constitution makes available to us the democratic processes by which the issues can be resolved. The final interpretation of the Constitution lies with the people, through processes provided by the framers of it.

We cannot settle the issues by use of inflamed tempers and heated arguments that excite prejudices and lead to violence. They will not be resolved by making them a political battleground.

The survival of our democratic processes and the Free World is at stake. If we divide ourselves Communist agitators almost certainly would take advantage of the opportunity to create chaos.

The issues, nevertheless, must be faced up to and not covered to fester and eat at the vitals of our democracy. But they must be faced in an atmosphere of calm and reason, without passion or hate and as Americans rather than Northerners and Southerners.

A Portrait of the Davidsons

An article touching on Soviet propaganda during the Cold War at a time when the newspapers were a primary source of news in America.

October 9, 1958

Red Mill in Washington

One of the four basic freedoms of our democracy, the freedom of the press, is being used in Washington in an open and avowed plot to destroy a form of government which protects that freedom.

The Russian government has brazenly moved into Washington a large corps of highly trained Communist propagandists for the purpose of influencing American officials and the public in favor of communism.

This red mill has for several weeks been misusing our freedom of the press to print and mail a huge volume of "press releases" from behind the closely guarded doors of the Soviet Embassy at 1706 18th St., N. W.

The Russians operate under all of the protections accorded our free press, but under none of the restraints that might subject them to libel action for their lies. Tons of this Communist propaganda are put into the mail at rates which require U. S. taxpayers to subsidize a part of the costs.

A Free Press

A call to the Russian Embassy to obtain an explanation brought the response that this is a "free country" and that the issuance of press releases by a foreign government was "perfectly legal," and besides what "is wrong with making the American people aware of our views?"

Why, then, we asked, does Moscow spend millions of rubles to jam our Voice of America broadcasts to the Russian people? There was a silence and then the phone clicked.

At the U. S. State Department we were told that we have made "diplomatic inquiry" of the Russian government whether we would be permitted to establish a similar propaganda agency in Moscow, but that no reply had been received.

Meanwhile, the red mill continues to operate full blast within sight of the White House under the same freedom granted the American press, but denied these same propagandists in their own country.

The Soft Touch

We have before us a typical "release" from the Russian Embassy press department. It is mimeographed on nine pages, single spaced. Embassy spokesmen refused to reveal how many names are on their mailing list.

The release follows closely the current "Moscow line." The objective seems to be to convince Americans that the 'peace-loving' Kremlin earnestly wants us to regard the Communists as close friends of America.

The lead "news item" features the "impressions" of a recent visitor to Russia, Adlai Stevenson. The story identifies him as "the leader of the Democratic party in the U. S. A. and reports that he was "deeply moved by the friendly attitude of the (Russian) people."

"Peace and friendship were the words he heard constantly," while in Russia, the release says. It adds that he left the Soviet Unions "filled with gratitude to the people of this great country," and that he had "no doubt that the people of Russia sincerely wished for peace and friendship."

What the release didn't say, but Mr. Stevenson did after returning is that he had some quite different impressions about the Russian dictators.

James A. Harding and the Potter Bible College

(Bowling Green, Kentucky) c. 1901

James A. Harding ("Uncle Jimmy") who founded the Potter Bible College where Clinton Davidson studied the Bible from 1901 to 1902, was an itinerant evangelist and preacher for most of his career. Harding had blazing blue eyes that could flash with earnestness or temper, but also weep with deep emotion during his preaching. He was "fiery, emotional, and inspirational. His magnetism and driving power were incentive enough to his students. His faith and zeal impressed every student who came under his sway." According to Richard T. Hughes, author of Reviving The Ancient Faith, Harding's convictions created a level of trust in God that awed and baffled many of his contemporaries. Although at one time he owned little more than two horses and a carriage, he was given the property in Bowling Green by the Potters including the school building, 140 acres and a two million dollar endowment (in today's currency) to start the Potter Bible College. The school eventually closed but the property continues over a hundred years later as Potter Ministries which serves as a home for orphans. Harding earned a degree from Bethany College in West Virginia, an institution started by Alexander Campbell.

(See History of the Restoration Movement in the References section.)

LINKS & REFERENCES

Other Books by Clinton Davidson
in the Library of Congress

THE LIFE INSURANCE TRUST
Prentice Hall, 1926

TOOL MONEY
Fiduciary Council, Inc., 1944

YOUR COST OF POSTWAR TAX PROPOSALS
Estimates of the Postwar Federal Budget
& Tax Rates Necessary to Balance It
Harding College, 1945

KEEPING PURCHASING POWER INTACT
Fiduciary Counsel, Inc. 1934

KEEPING FORTUNES INTACT
Fiduciary Counsel, Inc. 1932

• • •

A book which documents the influences of Clinton Davidson
in the history of the Churches of Christ in America.

REVIVING THE ANCIENT FAITH
by Richard T. Hughes

The Story of Churches of Christ in America

• • •

Camp Shiloh, the inner city youth program that
Clinton and Flora Davidson sponsored for many years at their Balbrook Estate
in New Jersey, continues to serve the N.Y.C. area with summer youth camps in
New York State.

SHILOH NYC
www.shilohnyc.org

Equipping Youth With Tools That Build Hope

• • •

A source with abundant information about the elders and history
of the Restoration Movement including James A. Harding and many others.

HISTORY OF THE RESTORATION MOVEMENT
www.therestorationmovement.com

• • •

A book Clinton Davidson kept on his desk
at Balbrook is a biography of his teacher at
Potter Bible College. J. N. Armstrong who became
the first president of Harding College in Searcy, Arkansas.

FOR FREEDOM
The Biography of J. N. Armstrong
by Lloyd Cline Sears

Published by Sweet Publishing Co. 1969

• • •

A book published in 1994 written by L. Edward Hicks
following the passing of George S. Benson.
This book explores in detail the impact of the NEP
on politics in America, the education of the new religious right,
and the influence of the NEP on the U.S. presidential election of 1980.

SOMETIMES IN THE WRONG,
BUT NEVER IN DOUBT

Published by The University of Tennessee Press

• • •

HARDING UNIVERSITY
www.harding.edu

Integrating Faith, Learning & Living

Book revision, cover, layout and scrapbook by

Michael Menes
(Great Grandson of Clinton Davidson)

Photo by Rebecca Menes

357 Darnit Rd. • Buckfield • Maine • 04220

msmenes@gmail.com

www.michaelmenes.com/publications/

Michael Menes
PUBLICATIONS

Made in the USA
Coppell, TX
17 November 2022